THE DAY THEY LOST THE H-BOMB

THE
DAY THEY LOST
THE H-BOMB

by Christopher Morris

COWARD-McCANN, Inc.
NEW YORK

Copyright ©1966 by Christopher Morris

FIRST AMERICAN EDITION 1966

Library of Congress Catalog
Card Number: 66-29688

PRINTED IN THE UNITED STATES OF AMERICA

To Georgina

Illustrations will be found following page 128.

CHAPTER ONE

THE GIANT B-52 bomber rumbled along the concrete runway, a healthy red glow belching from each of its eight powerful jet engines.

Ahead, the plane's dazzling lights illuminated the black zig-zag patterns of a thousand tyre burns inflicted by landing aircraft on the runway. Behind, a choking screen of dust and smoke was blasted skywards by the roaring thrust of the jets.

Hangars and buildings dotted around the airstrip of the Seymour Johnson base moulded into a blur as the lumbering Stratofortress swept by in the evening gloom.

The V1 speed – the maximum at which a plane can be braked to a safe stop in an emergency – had been reached. Now, beyond, was the point of no return.

At the cockpit controls the aircraft commander, Captain Charles F. Wendorf, firmly gripped the throttles. He gently eased back on the control wheel. The stubby nose of the plane responded by lifting into the air.

This was V2 – take-off speed. Majestically, and almost as if in slow motion, the B-52 climbed off the ground.

'Gear up!' ordered the pilot. Major Larry G. Messinger, the third pilot, squeezed the gear handle which hydraulically lifted the belly and nose wheels into the fuselage.

A red light flashed on, casting eerie shadows on the tense faces in the cabin. It indicated the landing gear was working perfectly and coming up. Captain Wendorf was now flying by instruments alone, his gaze concentrated on a mass of gauges, switches, levers, buttons and dials on the panel in front of him. He assessed the airspeed, rate of climb and direction.

Alongside him the co-pilot, First Lieutenant Michael Rooney, double-checked readings on his instrument panel, and at the captain's order 'zero flaps' leaned forward to push the flap handle to the neutral position. A needle flickered on the control panel to indicate the wing flaps were retracting from an angle of

9

twenty degrees to zero position, reducing the plane's lift but increasing its speed.

Far below the B-52 was a carpet of lights winking up from the houses strung around the base, headquarters of the 68th Bomber Wing at Goldsboro in North Carolina.

Another flight of the Strategic Air Command was safely airborne. Destination: unknown.

The plane and its crew of seven – unlike the 24-hour global missions of most S.A.C. bombers which patrol the skies against an enemy attack from behind the Iron Curtain – was on its way to rehearse the delicate operation of refuelling in mid-air at a predetermined rendezvous.

But this was a flight destined to provoke world attention. It would eventually force Mr Robert McNamara, America's Secretary of Defence, to slash the costs of S.A.C.'s round-the-clock alert by £23 million a year. It brought about the realisation that America's B-52 bomber fleet was ridiculously out-of-date, and that in the event of a Third World War the role of a Stratofortress would be, by comparison, like pitting a peashooter against a cannon.

In just five and a half years of its duties the kingpin role in Western defence had been taken over by nuclear missiles. Most of the sky patrols were unnecessary and could have been scrapped long before the stinging lesson provided by Captain Wendorf's flight.

His rendezvous point – with a KC-135 jet tanker aircraft – was to be at 30,500 feet, off the south east Mediterranean coast of Spain.

His cargo was top secret.

For hours, the huge aircraft flew on serenely until the uneventful night melted into pale dawn sunlight and the B-52 approached the Spanish coast.

And a place called Palomares.

*   *   *

Monday morning, January 17, 1966, was a special day for the 1,200 villagers who were planning a fiesta in Palomares. It was their big day of the year, the day of Saint Anton the Abbot. That evening, the wine would flow as they gaily celebrated the memory of the venerated hermit, Saint Anton, said by legend to have died in A.D. 356 at the age of 105.

Palomares – it is so tiny it was wiped off most maps of Spain over 200 years ago – is in the province of Almeria. The region was ruled by the Moors for 700 years and their influence still remains. Many Arabian names like Benahadux, Canjayar, Mojacar, Laujar and Almeria itself – derived from the Arabian 'Al-bahri', mirror of the sea – have survived to the present day. Some villages still look more Moroccan than Spanish with their low, crumbling, cubic and whitewashed houses resembling, in the distance, a cluster of sugar lumps.

Truly, Palomares is a village lost in time, where the 20th century has been cruel to its inhabitants. It prospered as an important iron and zinc mining district until the 1920s, when the lode was exhausted and all but a few of the residents left to seek a better life.

The village is perched on a hillock, half-a-mile from the blue-green sea. The beaches and weather are incomparable. Swelling sands roll as far as the eye can see. The sun shines brilliantly all year round from a cloudless blue sky. In eight years villagers claim it has rained only once.

Incredibly, there has not yet (1966) been an invasion by tourists. This north western outpost of the Costa del Sol has still to be discovered. Holidaymakers, of course, like comforts and at present Palomares has no tarmac roads, no running water, no telephones, no hotels, and only one television set.

Inevitably, the area is ear-marked for quick commercialisation. Nearly a billion pesetas is being invested in a vast 'Tourist City' on the nearby Puerto Rey beach with hotels, apartment blocks, restaurants, parking lots, bars and a cinema.

But for the time being the landscape, strikingly massive and rugged, remains unspoiled. Eroded mountain peaks as high as 8,400 feet level off to wide deserts that support no life.

The few riverbeds – like the dried-up Rio Almanzora alongside Palomares – provide fertile ground for luxurious orchards of oranges and lemons, and fields of grape vines, lush melons, tomatoes, onions and string beans.

In this dry and dusty area most of the farming has to be done without irrigation. The people tend to group themselves to-gether in settlements of farmhouses. In many places where the

heat is so intense, they live in caves, a tattered blanket strung up
to shade the entrance. The smarter caves have wooden doors with
bolts, even windows, cut into the rock for a room with a view.

Life is tough, poverty a prevalent fear. Only the fruit-growers
are assured of a steady income. Grain farming is virtually non-
existent for there is not enough rain for a good harvest.

Two miles further inland, along a bumpy cart-track rutted
by creaking wheels and pitted by the unshod hooves of donkeys
and mules, is the town of Vera. This is the shopping centre for
the villagers of Palomares.

Along a twisting coastal road, twenty-five miles to the north,
is the small fishing port of Aguilas. Another road that weaves
laboriously through the foothills of a mountain range leads to
Cuevas de Almanzora, then past an old Moorish fort to the
fishing village of Villaricos. This place, too, was once a go-ahead
mining settlement. Today, only the ruins of the mine buildings
remain with the sealed up shaft a few yards from the sea. The
dozen fishing boats are now relied upon to bring in sufficient
income for some of the hardier inhabitants who have remained.
Sardines, and 'langostinos' – crawfish – are the main catch, with
the luxury of an occasional lobster.

To the south of Palomares is Garrucha, another fishing port.
Then comes Mojacar, a village that nestles on top of a small
pyramid-like hill, the last stronghold of the Arabs in Spain
where many of the women are still veiled. Beyond, fifteen miles
along a coast road that frequently peters out and past film locations where sequences for 'Lawrence of Arabia' and 'Cleopatra'
were shot, lies Carboneras, once a booming mining centre.

At 10.0 a.m. that fateful Monday in Palomares, Senor Pedro
Ramirez, a 41-year-old tomato grower, was at work in the fields.
Meticulously he inspected row after row of plants in search of
crop-destroying insects that could cause him financial ruin.
Everything was fine. The green fruit, in some cases tinged red
with ripeness, hung heavily from the vivid green plants. Soon
they would be ready for picking. It would be time for packing
them carefully into wooden crates aboard trucks for eventual
export to England, France and Germany.

Ramirez, burly, gruff-spoken and wearing a patched brown
corduroy suit, stained green shirt and with a black beret on his
head at a jaunty angle, was typical of the hard-working men in

the village. He had his little tomato patch, a long-eared donkey, a rickety cart and a sparsely-furnished but comfortable little house. He was happy.

Another tomato grower, Miguel Castro, 37, his face deeply bronzed by the blistering sun, was feeding his six black and white cows in a shed next to his neat, whitewashed farmhouse. He hummed a Spanish pop song he had heard frequently on his transistor radio.

In the local bar, Jose Moreno finished off polishing the rows of bottles of cognac, whisky, gin, anis and champagne which he proudly displayed on a shelf. He then poured farmer Jose Portillo, 35, another large glass of local red wine and commented: 'There will be excellent crops this year.'

The farmer nodded agreement, downed the wine in a gulp, and after promising to return for the Saint Anton celebrations that evening, strode off to his fields to continue work.

Down a narrow twisting street, past the old grey-stoned village hall, was the school. Inside, the young schoolmaster, Jose Molerino, chalk in hand, was addressing his class of 52 elementary pupils, all boys, in his distinctive Andalusian dialect. The lesson was arithmetic and the boys looked bored. Soon, thank goodness, it would be 10.30 am. – time for a break.

The time, in fact, was just 10.10 a.m.

In nearby Vera, Captain Isidoro Calin, of the Guardia Civil – rural police – was at his desk awaiting a phone call to Almeria while carefully sifting through the morning's mail.

Meanwhile, out at sea from the port of Aguilas, 46-year-old Francisco Simo, shielding his eyes from the glare of the sun, was at the helm of his 66-foot fishing smack, the Manuela Orts Simo. It was a routine trip for the skipper and his crew of 7 who had fished the waters for 17 years. They had been out with their nets since 5 a.m. Soon it would be time for an early lunch and a siesta.

On the hilltop at Mojacar in a white-washed Moorish-style villa, blonde Mrs Helen Norland, 31, nursed year-old baby Ben. There was plenty of house-work to be done. She tucked the baby in his cot and prepared to start.

Then, suddenly, she heard it. The noise; the echoing whistle and roar of jet planes above.

Every morning at this time – 10.15 a.m. on the dot – she and her husband Till, a bearded 31-year-old artist, would hear the planes.

'They are better than having an alarm clock,' she reflected. 'Always dead on time. I watch them overhead every day, refuelling and flying so close together it's a miracle they do not crash.' She wondered about the mysteries of the air.

The villagers of Palomares, too – Pedro Ramirez, Miguel Castro, Jose Moreno, Jose Portillo and Jose Molinero – regularly heard or saw the planes flitting through the sky as though tied together. Captain Calin could hear the noise in his bare office. Fisherman Simo would sometimes wave skywards and toot the ship's foghorn as they flew overhead.

All of them wondered, at one time or another, what would happen if there was a crash.

In seconds they were to find out.

*   *   *

A bleep on the radar screen alerted the B-52's navigator, Captain Ivan Buchanan, of the approaching aircraft. In a few minutes the tricky mid-air refuelling operation would be attempted.

That morning two U.S. bombers – their 10,000 miles range fuel loads nearly half-exhausted – were scheduled to rendezvous off the Spanish coast nearly six miles up with two KC-135 tanker aircraft.

The bleeps on the screen now numbered three. All aircraft were preparing for the manoeuvre.

The commander, Captain Wendorf, disengaged the levers of the automatic pilot of his B-52, releasing for manual control the ailerons to bank and turn the plane, the elevators on the tail stabilizers for up and down movement, and the rudder which steadied turns. The bomber handled smoothly and there was practically no air turbulence; ideal conditions.

One of the silver, four-jet tankers – the military version of the Boeing 707 commercial airliner – would soon be visible through the cockpit windows. But Captain Wendorf had no time to admire the glorious view. He closely studied the instrument panel readings.

First Lieutenant Steven G. Montanus, the radio navigator, was now in contact with the rendezvous plane.

The KC-135 was attached to the 910th Air Refuelling

Squadron at Bergstrom Air Force Base, near Austin, Texas. Less than an hour earlier the plane had taken off from the joint Spanish-American base at Torrejon, on the outskirts of Madrid, headquarters in Spain of the US 16th Air Force and Strategic Air Command.

Major Emil T. Chapla, commander of the jet tanker, was a skilled veteran of flight refuelling. He had a crew of three, co-pilot Captain Paul R. Lane, navigator Captain Leo E. Simmons, and boom operator Master Sergeant Lloyd G. Potolicchio, whose job it was to direct the extending, telescope-like fuel boom from underneath the tail of the tanker to the intake cone of the B-52 situated at the front of the bomber's fuselage.

The two giants of the air were being slowly drawn together as if by an invisible magnet. Lieutenant Rooney, the co-pilot, calculated the estimated ground speed of the aircraft at about 365 knots.

Major Messinger, the third pilot, had computed the exact amount of fuel used and the total required to be pumped through the boom.

All systems, in space-age jargon, were 'go'. Both planes were lined up for refuelling, a manoeuvre which, at the best of times, demanded finely concentrated skill and precision from the two pilots involved.

The jet tanker levelled-off at about 150 feet above the huge B-52, flying directly in front. Like an overfed python the boom snaked out slowly from beneath the KC-135 towards the intake cone of the bomber. It was suspended at a 45 degrees angle by the terrific rushing force of wind, curving slightly under the strain.

Finally, contact! The nozzle of the boom was snapped into the cone, and mechanically locked. The operation of feeding out the boom and fixing it had taken less than five minutes.

Now came the actual refuelling and the pumping began. Everything was going smoothly. The exact time: 10.11 a.m.

Both planes was nearing the Spanish coast, headed north westwards inland. Inside the B-52's cockpit, Captain Wendorf momentarily glanced upwards through the window at the tanker above. Simultaneously a red warning light flashed on in the cockpit.

'Engine on fire!' co-pilot Rooney shouted across.

Strapped in their seats on the flight deck none of the crew could actually observe the licking flames, fanned by the airstream, spurting from a starboard engine. But the pilot could evaluate only too well the ominous warning flashed on the instrument panel. He knew immediately which of the eight engines was on fire. He cut its fuel supply, and pressed a button operating the built-in fire extinguishers.

Lieutenant Montanus was frantically radioing an emergency alert to his opposite number, Captain Simmons, in the KC-135.

'Fire! Haul up the boom!'

Too late. There was a muffled explosion from the blazing engine of the B-52. With a terrifying roar flames engulfed part of the wing section near the fuselage and shot hungrily towards the intake cone where hundreds of gallons of highly inflammable fuel were still being pumped.

Major Chapla, pilot of the jet tanker, tense and with his face beaded with sweat, realised they were virtually suspended and trapped in the crater of a volcano about to erupt.

Boom operator Potolicchio, from his perch under the tail, cried out in horror. He was the only man of the 11 aboard the two planes able to witness the drama of the stricken bomber.

He could clearly see jagged, fiery lumps of metal peeling off the B-52's wing and then slowly spiralling earthwards, trailing white smoke. They made macabre patterns in the blue sky not unlike those painted by jets for an awed public at an air show exhibition.

'She's going to explode!'

Captain Simmons had already radioed their desperate plight to Strategic Air Command headquarters at Torrejon airbase.

The second B-52 and KC-135 aircraft, some three miles distant, had not yet begun their refuelling operation. The shocked crews were powerless to help, able only to watch the enlarging sinister smoke trail from the burning bomber, and the struggle of the two planes, seemingly waltzing a dance of death in the sky.

Two hundred miles away at the Spanish-U.S. Moron base, near Seville, a siren was already blaring the alert for take-off to the crews of a C-54 – specially equipped for air-sea rescue work with a disaster unit aboard – and a T-39 twin-jet reconnaissance aircraft.

At Torrejon, Major General Delmar Wilson, Commander of
the 16th Air Force, was notified. He raced to the radar controllers and communications centre.

By now the two planes were less than a mile from the Spanish
coastline. The time: 10.22 a.m.

Acrid fumes were seeping into the cockpit of the bomber as
the fire raged hopelessly out of control. Captain Wendorf had
to make a split second decision. To attempt flying on to Moron
for a crash landing? To ditch in the Mediterranean? Or to bale
out?

Moron was really out of the reckoning. It was too far away.
In any case, it would be dangerous piloting a blazing bomber
over the towns and villages of southern Spain, however sparsely
populated. And particularly as the plane was carrying secret
armament aboard.

Ditching in the sea seemed the likeliest escape from total
disaster.

'Jettison armaments!' came the hoarse, curt instruction over
the inter-com.

The gunner, Technical Sergeant Ronald P. Snyder, watched
the huge doors of the armament bay swing open menacingly.
But at this precise moment another violent blast racked the
tortured fuselage of the B-52.

And amid the blinding smoke, hailing debris of fatigued,
crunched metal and searing fire the bomber and the KC-135
appeared to collide. Both planes momentarily lurched to a halt,
suspended like two broken puppet dolls.

Barely a second later both plummeted into dizzying dives of
death, spinning grotesquely, shedding off fragments of twisted
steel, and casting a pall of smoke to obliterate the morning
sun.

'Bale out!'

Captain Wendorf stubbed his thumb on the ejection seat firing
button. There was a bang and a stinging pain shot through his
right arm. Instinctively, he tried to clutch his shoulder. The blue
sky turned green, mauve, pink and orange all at once. There
was a peculiar ringing in his ears. He passed out.

Below the spiralling aircraft, a blur of land and sea was rushing up fast. Co-pilot Rooney ejected from the crippled plane.
Over and over he tumbled.

Captain Buchanan, the radar navigator, felt the cold rush of air as his ejection seat blasted clear.

'The parachute!'

Still strapped to the seat, pinioned by gravity forces as he shot earthwards, Captain Buchanan realised to his horror that the parachute – his only hope of survival – was slung under the cushioned chair. Was it still there? Desperately he groped downwards for the harness. His fingers clawed frantically under the seat. Dizzily he continued the plunge in space as the bulky seat propelled its human cargo faster towards doom.

It *was* there!

Captain Buchanan dragged the harness out from beneath the seat, and feverishly fought exhaustion and the freezing cold of descent to strap it on. His face contorted. The ground seemed so near it would swallow him up. He could almost reach out and touch it.

Major Messinger, the third pilot, felt the searing heat. His body was numbed, yet his mind alertly battled against the physical lack of response. 'Must get out of here!'

There was another dull explosion. Its force hurled the major out into the sky. He was barely conscious. Blood streaked from a gash over his right eye, temporarily blinding him. He had left it too late to press the ejection seat button. The world whirled below and came to meet him. His parachute was strapped on and he pulled the cord.

The flames now crackled hungrily over the aircraft's cabin. In seconds, electronics warfare officer, First Lieutenant George T. Glesner, and radio navigator Montanus, would be trapped. Montanus coolly transmitted a final distress call. Almost simultaneously he and Glesner ejected. The seats fell away and they pulled the ripcord tags. Red and white silk billowed out. But tongues of orange flame licked at the silk. As the 'chutes drifted down their human pendulums gazed fearfully upwards at singeing, ever-widening circular gaps in them. The parachutes gained momentum with every milli-second.

Like a wounded giant eagle in its death throes the B-52, scattering blazing wreckage in its wake, hurtled to final destruction. Mangled lumps of white-hot metal rained into the sea, sending up spouts of water amid hissing steam, choking smoke and bubbles. Incandescent chunks of steel slammed into the parched earth with such force that they were buried from sight. Scattered over a vast area of land were charred sections of the fuselage, electronic equipment, ejection seats, a twisted, smouldering wing section, and slashed, punctured wheels still aimlessly rotating among the landing gear. The engines, torn from their structures under the wings and spewing flaming black and red jet fuel, roared earthwards like fireballs. Afterwards, oily black smoke rose from the gaping craters blasted in the soil where some had landed.

Overhead the stricken KC-135 jet tanker spun crazily. It appeared to leapfrog over an obstructing palm tree and then, with an explosion that rocked the ground, crashed in a horror of dust, smoke and flames.

At Torrejon, radio contact with Lieutenant Montanus on the B-52 and Captain Simmons on the refuelling plane had cut dead shortly after messages that they were baling out.

In those short seconds the blue sky had turned black. It had rained fire and destruction. Soon the terrible consequences would be known and feared.

*   *   *

At precisely 10.22 a.m. a young British holidaymaker, Eddie Fowlie, was strolling along the deserted beach at Carboneras, some 15 miles from Palomares. Casually, he had been taking random snapshots with his expensive, single lens reflex camera.

Photography was his hobby, but these were just the usual unspectacular holiday pictures for the family album; of the distant shimmering hills across a rutted, desert-like piece of land with its one solitary olive tree; of a shepherd boy and his shaggy black and white collie dog guiding over 100 sheep along a cart-track.

Eddie Fowlie hadn't really taken much notice of the whistling jets above. But, by instinct, he pointed the 55 mm. lens of his camera skywards.

In that instant the spot where the two planes had been flying so close together vanished in a pall of white smoke that mushroomed high above the ocean. A second later came a terrific explosion.

Eddie Fowlie clicked the shutter of his camera. It was so far away he didn't really expect anything to show on the negative. So he slung the camera over his shoulder and from his position, sitting astride a white-washed wall, shaded his eyes to witness the drama of the two crashing aircraft.

'I could see wreckage of both planes falling down into the sea. Then I noticed parachutes billowing open. Some were those of the crew but apparently there was some equipment and other strange-looking objects suspended under the other parachutes,' he explained. 'They splashed into the sea, but I could not see if they were rescued as a hill was obscuring my view. I ran to try and get help.'

Three weeks later Eddie Fowlie collected his developed film. It had come out well. Quite clearly, negative number 12 showed the smoke trail of one of the jets and the heart-shaped white cloud resulting from the impact of the two aircraft.

It was the only photograph of the actual collision. A snap-shot for which the French magazine *Paris Match* was later to pay him over £100 when their reporters, Monique Valls and Vick Vance, learned of the picture and drove to his holiday villa to buy the roll of film.

At sea, the skipper of the Dutch motor vessel William Koerts reported the collision to Spanish coastal radio stations. Similar reports were soon made by at least five other ships in the area. They all joined in a mass, sweeping search after first steaming to the rescue of any possible survivors.

From the gently swaying deck of his boat, fisherman Francisco Simo, burly and sun-bronzed, also observed the collision. So did most of his seven crew members who had been busily sorting out the early morning catch and checking their still-dripping nets for gashes or tears.

They rushed to line the deck rails of the little brown and cream painted vessel as it bobbed on the restless Mediterranean swell. They heard the explosion, saw the cloud of smoke and stared into the blueness for signs of any survivors parachuting down.

'Senor, it was terrible. We all prayed for the men in those planes,' fisherman Simo later recounted. 'I had a strange feeling that morning that something bad was going to happen.

'Every day, at about the same time, we would hear the jets overhead. Some days it was so clear we could almost read the letters and numbers painted on their wings.

'But there was a haze that morning. It was difficult to see exactly what happened. The planes were very close. There was a trail of smoke pouring from the engines of the big plane behind. Both aircraft veered together. Then we all heard the big bang. Si, senor, it was truly terrible.'

Simo inhaled deeply on his loosely-rolled cigarette with its foul-smelling tobacco. 'We first saw several red and white parachutes of the planes' crew members. One of them burned up before landing.

'Then, minutes later, a striped white parachute landed about 80 yards from my boat. There was a light blue object about five feet long attached to it. It landed in the water and sank immediately. This was very curious. I had no idea what it might be.

'Some seconds afterwards another, much bigger parachute, greyish in colour, splashed down near the boat and at first I thought there was a man hanging from it. It fell much more slowly than the red and white parachutes of the crew. But as soon as it hit the water it also sank.'

The little fishing vessel was about five miles from the coast. The craggy outline of the mountain range loomed through the haze. Fisherman Simo made a mental note of the boat's position, then grabbed the helm.

'Rapido, amigos!' he yelled.

The motor chugged noisily towards where the first red and white parachute had fallen. A bright marker dye was spreading around the spot, like red ink on blue blotting paper.

One of the 'chutes billowed on the surface with an airman hopelessly entangled in its cords. He was being slowly tugged through the icy water as he struggled to unbuckle the harness. Of the other parachutes there was no sign and Simo peered through his powerful German binoculars, scanning the sea. Over the brooding swell he could just make out the form of another survivor, apparently unconscious, but floating in his dark flight overalls and orage-coloured inflated life-jacket.

Other little fishing boats of the Aguilas fleet joined the Manuela Orts Simo, hurriedly changing course, to reach the spot. Rescue was at hand for three of the B-52's crew.

Just one hour later a tiny flotilla swept urgently into the

harbour at Aguilas. Two white ambulances waited on the quay-side. So did nearly 500 fisherfolk. Word had spread quickly after Simo's radio message. Wrapped in blue blankets the three airmen were placed on stretchers and gingerly lifted from the boats to the shore. Seconds later the ambulances, their sirens wailing, raced through narrow winding streets to the Hospital de Caridad, where doctors were already waiting.

Captain Wendorf, the pilot, First Lieutenant Rooney, the co-pilot, and Major Messinger, the third pilot, were the lucky ones. They had had fantastic escapes with only slight injuries.

'After I blacked out I was unconscious until I hit the water,' said the captain. 'The coldness sooned revived me. I splashed around for a bit then I could see the bows of a small boat ploughing through the sea towards me.

'I was almost all in. My right arm was killing me.'

When co-pilot Rooney landed in the water the giant parachute cascaded on top of him. He tried desperately to propel himself clear of the shrouds only to become trapped and tangled in the harness.

'What a relief it was when I heard the throbbing motor of an approaching vessel. I felt sore all over and wasn't sure if I was still in one piece.'

Major Messinger knew he was safe even before he was dumped into the sea. Swinging underneath the folds of his parachute he could see at least three tiny boats below.

'I tugged at the harness to direct the splash-down as near to one of them as possible. The sea was quite a shaker. I'd always believed the Mediterranean was beautifully warm. It was freezing!'

In the hospital, while they awaited transfer to the clinic at Torrejon, the doctors diagnosed their injuries: Wendorf, a fractured right arm; Rooney, lacerations of the buttocks; Messinger, lacerations above the right eye and severe bruising of the left leg.

Military chiefs in Madrid phoned through strict instructions to the hospital that none of the survivors was to talk to anyone about the crash.

*   *   *

On the hilltop at Mojacar the explosion rattled the sun shutters and even a lump of plaster dislodged and tumbled from an old crack in the ceiling of the Norland villa.

Mrs Helen Norland, a former fashion photographer, was pegging the Monday morning washing on the rope line in the garden. Her husband was busily engaged dabbing oils with a long-handled artist's brush on to his latest canvas, a vivid landscape painting of the view from the tiny living-room where he had set up his easel.

Ironically, the young couple had recently quit their home in London, fed-up with the hum-drum of city life, in search of some peace and quiet.

'I knew something was wrong when I noticed the two planes flying so close together. I had never seen them that close before,' recalled Mrs Norland. 'When they collided it was just like a bomb going off. My husband rushed into the garden and we both saw a cloud of smoke, rather like a big white balloon, enlarging in the sky.

'Then the wreckage started raining down. At first I thought it was going to land near our village but most of it fell in the sea or by the beach at Palomares. A few seconds later we saw some parachutes opening out. There was a fairly strong breeze blowing and they drifted a long way out to sea.'

As soon as he heard the aerial bang Captain Calin rushed from his desk, untidily heaped with documents, into the courtyard outside the Guardia Civil 'cuartel' – quarters – at Vera. His shiny black patent leather tricorn hat glinted in the sunlight as he peered skywards.

'Terrible. Terrible,' he muttered, gripping the breast pockets of his smart olive green uniform. 'I must alert the hospital in case there are any survivors. Sargento!'

A policeman nearby clicked his heels to attention. 'Round up some men. Wherever that wreckage falls there may be some survivors. They will need help. Hurry sergeant!'

*　　*　　*

At Palomares it was as though the gates of Hell had suddenly swung open.

One minute it was peaceful. Crickets chattered contentedly

in the long alfalfa grass, black and white goats grazed by the sun-splashed village square, women knelt over washboards busily scrubbing while others fed clucking chickens or pottered around with their household chores. Their menfolk sweated in the fields with their beloved crops or stole into Jose Moreno's bar for a quick chat and hasty dash of cognac.

The next minute came the explosion more terrifying than a clap of thunder. The sun was blotted out. Uncanny was the silence that briefly followed.

Then, as the terrible rain of fire began to descend, women fled to the safety of their little white houses slamming behind them thick oak studded doors. The goats and other terrified animals – cats, dogs, donkeys, mules, sheep and even cows – bolted through the streets. The men ran from the fields, along the maze of paths and up the slope towards the village, trying to reach cover before the wreckage tumbled down.

Women's cries echoed in the air. 'It is the end of the world!' 'We will all be killed!' 'God protect us!'

The boys in the recently-constructed school building huddled in fear over their desks, clapping their hands to their ears as the screams of the falling jets whistled deafeningly closer and closer.

Father Navarete, the village priest, at the doorway of the tiny church, grasped a Bible and mouthed a silent prayer.

Pedro Ramirez hid in a little shed near his tomato fields and looked out. 'A huge column of black smoke spiralled over the village. Then huge lumps of wreckage slammed into the ground. There was fire everywhere. I was too scared to move. If I had run away I might have been killed. One lump of metal landed only a short distance from the shed.'

Miguel Castro managed to reach his farmhouse safely. From a vantage point in the adjoining barn, where he garaged an ancient tractor, he watched the crash horror. He said:

'It reminded me of the bomb raids during the Spanish Civil War 30 years ago. The ground shuddered as the flaming wreckage landed. One plane skimmed over the rooftops and a few seconds after it had disappeared from sight over a hilltop in the direction of Cuevas de Almanzora there was a terrific explosion.'

Part of the B-52's landing gear fell less than 50 feet away from the home of Senora Fernanda Quinilla, 55, and her farmer husband. A pair of giant rubber tyres protruded, their supporting mechanism buried deep in the ground.

'The sky was on fire and black smoke curled up from the ground. My daughter-in-law and I did not know where to run. We ducked under this small wall,' she said, pointing to a two-foot high balustrade in front of the farmhouse. 'We saw the fire around us and feared everything would explode.'

Jose Molinero, the schoolmaster, saw a blazing wing section crash into a field less than 100 feet away. As more flaming debris was raining down in the area another teacher, Pedro Sanchez, tried to calm the 52 boys.

'Don't panic! If we all stay in the school we will be safe. Let us have courage.'

He smiled assurance to hide his own fear. Some of the boys wanted to try and run from the school to their nearby homes. Pedro Sanchez prayed that his decision to make them remain was correct.

For ten terrible minutes the village sheltered in fear. Then a strange silence descended. The wary villagers emerged from their hiding places, pale and shaken, to assess the damage and toll. Trails of black and white smoke littered the sky. Charred wreckage was scattered in their fields. And they could hear the soft crackling of flames.

But, miraculously, not a single person had been killed, maimed, injured – or even scratched.

It was Father Navarete who was later to offer the simple explanation for their survival. 'You see, it was the day of our Patron Saint. He protected us. The people of Palomares, by their faith and beliefs, were saved by Saint Anton the Abbot. There can be no other solution.'

In little huddled groups the women gathered to talk in excited whispers of their incredible escapes. The men, many heaving buckets of water, together with some enterprising farmers who had shovelled sand on to their donkey carts, headed towards the fields to extinguish the dozens of fires and to see if they could rescue anyone who might have survived the holocaust.

Soon they were to be joined by police detachments who arrived by jeep from the Guardia Civil cuartel at Vera. Hundreds of people from miles around who had seen the planes crashing and heard the explosions descended on Palomares. Some were anxious to join the rescue work, others just wanted to satisfy their morbid curiosity and watch.

In the fields it was a grim scene. Wreckage had fallen over an area of 15 square miles. At the foot of the mountains a huge blackened hulk lay among tomato plants. It was the tail assembly of the bomber, the largest part left of the aircraft. Nearly a mile away was the twisted, still-burning wreckage of one of the KC-135's engines. Parts of the wing lay nearby among other unidentifiable chunks of metal. One hundred yards further on, with flames shooting nearly 100 feet in the air, was the lower part of the fuselage. It blazed for nearly five hours. The heat was so searing no one could get within 20 yards. And when the flames were finally put out, and only a blackened hulk remained, they dragged the bodies of Major Chapla, the pilot, and Master Sergeant Potolicchio, the boom operator, from the smouldering pyre.

Rescue workers also found the bodies of two of the B-52's crew – First Lieutenant Glesner, and radio navigator Montanus. They were horribly burned and were still wearing their parachute harnesses. There was little left to identify what had once been the red and white silk of their chutes, just charred material.

Radar navigator Buchanan, who had buckled on his harness in mid-air, was found slumped and apparently dead by the seashore. He was still strapped in his seat which, at the moment of impact, had landed on top of him.

But farmer Jose Portillo knelt down to feel his pulse. 'He's alive. Quick, somebody fetch the doctor.'

Gently, they cut the straps to release Captain Buchanan from the imprisoning seat. His eyes flickered open briefly. He tried to speak, but lapsed again into unconsciousness. His face was streaked with blood from cuts around the eyes. Otherwise, he appeared unharmed. It was an incredible escape. The nylon straps had saved his life when he was pitched out of the plane by trapping him in the seat, and thus enabling him to retrieve his parachute harness.

Later, at the clinic in Vera, he told how he had been unable to unbuckle the straps as he plummeted earthwards. 'I was falling at a tremendous speed. Even after I had managed to strap on the parachute and pull the ripcord I was still a prisoner in the seat. I struggled desperately to get free, but in vain.

'The heavy weight of the seat propelled me downwards at an

alarming rate. I realised that if I hit the ground at that speed I would probably be killed. I tried to guide the parachute so I would land near the beach. If I had splashed down into the sea I would have been dragged under and drowned. It was quite a predicament!'

Captain Buchanan was fortunate. He landed on comparatively soft ground near the sandy beach. His only injuries, apart from a cut right eye, were bruises on his right hand and left arm, sustained while trying to break his rapid fall.

Meanwhile, the grim hunt went on for three other airmen missing from the two planes. Among the thousands of pieces of wreckage a wrist watch was found. It had stopped at 10.22 a.m., revealing the exact time of the crash. But of the missing three – gunner Snyder, of the B-52, and co-pilot Lane and navigator Simmons, of the jet tanker – there was no trace. They were almost certainly dead, either drowned or blown to pieces in the explosion.

The gentle people of Palomares searched diligently for the missing airmen. But they found nothing and were soon ready to return to their normal, placid, easy-going routine. They were completely unaware of the reason for the dramatic events which were to follow and they neither sought nor desired the spotlight of world attention which was to focus upon them and their village.

They did not know that as a result of that mid-air collision they had come within a whisper of being blasted to eternity – along with half the population of South Western Europe – and that their lives and livelihoods were still threatened.

How could they know that in the armament-bay of that crashed B-52 had been four of the most powerful H-bombs in the world?

CHAPTER TWO

ON SEPTEMBER 26, 1953, Spain – for so many years branded as an outcast in Europe following its bloody 1936–39 Civil War in which a million died – took its first faltering steps on a pathway to restore prestige.

On that day, an agreement was signed between the Secretary of State, the late Mr John Foster Dulles, and the former Spanish Foreign Minister, Senor Alberto Martin Artajo, giving the United States the right to use military installations on the Iberian peninsular in exchange for dollars and military support that would help Spain to put its economy back on its feet.

The pact also signified the beginning of the end of an international boycott clamped down by the United Nations on Spain, because of its wartime ties with the axis countries, in 1946.

So the Strategic Air Command came to Spain, with bases at Torrejon, 15 miles east of Madrid, at Zaragoza, halfway between the Spanish capital and Barcelona, and at Moron, near Seville, in the south west.

In addition the Americans built a huge Polaris submarine base at Rota, on the south west coast, and several naval depots and radar sites scattered throughout the country. The number of U.S. military, including dependents, stationed in Spain was estimated at close to 25,000.

America generously pumped one and a half billion dollars into Spain; one third was for the cost of construction of the bases, one third was for economic aid and the rest came in loans. And Spain's economy, for years plagued with inflationary tendencies, prospered.

The bases agreement was set for a period of ten years. Before it expired, however, and knowing the importance America attached to the alliance, Generalissimo Francisco Franco pounced on the opportunity of securing vastly increased political recognition for his régime in the West. The 73-year-old Spanish dictator shrewdly declared that the new world strategy made revision of the agreement with the U.S. necessary.

So the new Foreign Minister, Senor Fernando Maria Castiella y Maiz, notified the American government of Spain's intention to seek a renegotiation of the pact. It was bluntly pointed out that in 10 years the ever-present threat of a missile attack, particularly with U.S. striking forces occupying the bases, made Spain more vulnerable than before. Franco wanted a bigger say in decisions concerning Western defence planning. Whatever the plans of President Charles de Gaulle of France, regarding the North Atlantic Treaty Organisation and his independent atomic force, Spain was sticking by Washington.

And Franco won the day. The agreement was renewed for another five years with continued economic aid, and with the promise of establishing a bilateral consultative committee on defence matters.

A joint declaration, signed by the Spanish Foreign Minister and the Secretary of State, Dean Rusk, said: 'The U.S. government reaffirms its recognition of the importance of Spain to the security, well-being and development of the Atlantic and Mediterranean areas.

'The two governments recognise that the security and integrity of both Spain and the United States are necessary for the common security. A threat to either country, and to the joint facilities that each provides for the common defence, would be a matter of common concern to both countries and each country would take such action as it may consider appropriate within the framework of its constitutional processes.'

The renewal of the pact certainly gave Spain new authority in Western alliance defence matters, short of actual membership in N.A.T.O. And the Strategic Air Command was in Spain to stay.

*　　　*　　　*

The United States Air Force had always refused, for security reasons, to disclose exactly how many war planes were kept in the air at any one time by S.A.C., but the B-52 bomber force consisted of 600 aircraft.

These whispering giants patrolled the northern skies day and night on constant alert against an enemy attack. Usually, each plane was loaded with nuclear bombs, enough to flatten any city in the world.

From 1959 the United States had kept 300 aircraft on a 15-minute alert in the East-West cold war, at a staggering cost of more than £37 million a year.

An unspecified number of them had always been in the air. The routes they flew were strictly hush-hush, but it was known that they patrolled mainly the northern half of the globe, and especially those routes which the Soviet Union would be most likely to use in launching a missile attack against America.

An even more closely guarded secret was the type and number of bombs each plane carried and their destructive capacity. But, as the US intended them as second strike weapons, it could be safely accepted that their power of destruction was more than adequate to inflict crippling blows.

The question as to whether Captain Wendorf had charge of nuclear warheads in the bomb bay of his ill-fated B-52 was one about which the world would soon demand an answer.

*   *   *

A tree-lined dual highway sweeps majestically out of Madrid towards the Torrejon airbase. It is a fast road, not without its fatalities among personnel driving back after a Saturday night out in the Spanish capital.

But once the ordeal of escaping from the traffic snarl-ups in the Paseo de la Castellana and Avenida de America, and from the sweating, whistle-blowing policemen and impatiently honking taxis has been achieved, it is only a brisk 15-minute drive to the base.

Madrid is a city with practically no suburbs. Once the tightly-packed skyscraper apartments have been passed it is almost open countryside, although an industrial boom heralds the construction of film studios, motels, and a score of factories along this road which goes on to Barcelona, a ten-hour drive away.

The base lies almost alongside Madrid's Barajas international airport, two miles from the dusty village of Torrejon de Ardoz which, despite the American invasion thirteen years ago, still retains a typical Spanish charm. The villagers have resisted urges to open hamburger bars, bowling alleys or nightclubs.

Yet they have become accustomed to the wailing klaxons alerting air crews, and the deafening roar of jets climbing overhead.

Torrejon (1966) is the nerve centre for all Strategic Air Command operations in Spain.

During the early years of the U.S.-Spanish alliance, nuclear-armed B-47 bombers nestled on their concrete pads at the base like giant missiles aimed at a distant enemy. Armed guards and barbed wire surrounded them.

When the klaxons sounded, mechanics rushed from their trailer homes near the bombers and prepared to start the jets. Within seconds jeeps screeched to a halt with the three-man flight crews.

They did not know if it was just an alert or the start of a nuclear war. The bombers rolled down the 13,400-foot runway all set to strike against long-assigned targets in the Soviet Union. They rarely took off. Always the warning was radioed through at the last second that it was merely another practice run.

This S.A.C. 'Reflex' operation – forced by Russian air, missile and nuclear progress – went on relentlessly.

The B-47 bombers were replaced mainly by the longer-range B-52s which carried out the 24-hour global patrols while the world worked and slept, and which could be refuelled in flight.

Torrejon was originally designated to handle a wing of 45 bombers, a squadron of 15 tanker aircraft and a squadron of 25 interceptors. The Americans acknowledged, however, that Russia might strike first in Spain and knock out the three S.A.C. bases. Hence, a flock of F-100 jet fighters took over to comprise the main airborne force at the base. A squadron of tankers remained, but the B-52s, in general, were kept in the United States, safer from attack.

On January 17, Major General Wilson, Commander of the U.S. 16the Air Force at Torrejon, whose tour of duty in Spain was drawing to a close, was reading the daily reports when he was informed of the refuelling B-52 with its engine on fire. The tall, burly general was a popular commander and had a brilliant 30 years service record as a flying officer. He was in combat in Europe with the 8th Air Force and took part in the initial B-29 strikes against Japan from Saipan. He worked with General

LeMay for the Atom Bomb Project in the South Pacific area. Important assignments took him to the Pentagon, the Air University and commands in the U.S., England and, finally, Torrejon in 1964.

When radio contact with the B-52 and the KC-135 jet tanker was lost that morning General Wilson knew he faced a crisis. From the red-bricked radar controllers and communications centre, orders went out for a briefing of senior officers.

The atmosphere in the crowded briefing room at the base was both stuffy and tense. The assembled officers listened attentively under the harsh glare of the neon lights as General Wilson pointed towards the large map of Spain pinned to the wall.

'Palomares is approximately here, gentlemen,' he explained, stabbing a finger in the direction of a red circle painted roughly on the map. 'It is my intention to set up a camp somewhere near the village, probably by the beach. I cannot emphasise too strongly that this operation must be carried out with the utmost security. Is that clearly understood?'

Colonel Barnett 'Skippy' Young, Torrejon's Information Officer, nodded an acknowledgement. The General mopped his perspiring brow and concluded with another warning: 'After our initial survey this may turn out to be a lengthy operation.'

Then, with a curt 'That will be all!', he strode briskly from the room to make his own preparations for departure to Palomares, along with 100 airmen.

Meanwhile, messages were being flashed to service chiefs in Europe and America after confirmation of the crash had been radioed by the crews of the second circling B-52 and KC-135 aircraft.

In Europe, the Commander-in-Chief of the U.S. Air Force, General Bruce K. Halloway, was notified at Wiesbaden, Germany. So, too, was Allied Supreme Commander, General Lyman Lemnitzer, at his headquarters, S.H.A.P.E., in Paris.

In Madrid the Spanish Air Minister, Lieutenant General Jose Lacalle Larraga, and the American ambassador, Mr Angier Biddle Duke, were informed. And at his gun-guarded Pardo Palace, amid the sweet-smelling pine trees 10 miles from the city, Generalissimo Franco grimly received the news.

In America there was uproar among military chiefs at the Pentagon – 'a flap of the highest order' according to one general

– and Secretary of Defence Mr McNamara was alerted. At the White House in Washington a phone rang urgently. President Lyndon B. Johnson lifted the receiver. . . .

Other sorts of messages were already being flashed around the world from the Spanish capital. Inevitably, foreign correspondents had picked up sparse details of the crash.

But it was a tentative bulletin from United Press International, date-lined Almeria, which first alerted the world 'outside' to the magnitude of the Palomares story. It said: 'Two US Air Force planes – one of them a B-52 *possibly carrying a nuclear bomb* – collided in the air over the south east coast of Spain during a refuelling mission today.'

Well, *was* there an atomic bomb or a hydrogen warhead aboard the B-52?

The US Air Force clamped a security blanket around the collision. Colonel Young remembered the orders of the briefing. 'I cannot answer any questions about that subject,' was his stock answer to enquiries about the bomber's mystery cargo.

'No comment!'

* * *

Four o'clock in the afternoon and Palomares awoke from its fitful siesta.

Nearly six hours had elapsed since the multi-million dollar crash horror. Overhead buzzed two reconnaissance aircraft. The twin-jet T-39 from Moron airbase, like a circling vulture about to swoop on its prey, carried out an extensive aerial survey of the areas where still-smoking and charred wreckage lay on the ground below. A tiny spotter plane, the single-engined 2-U, zoomed above the tomato fields taking photographs.

The C-54 rescue plane lumbered ceaselessly across the skies far out above the Mediterranean. Occasionally, the pilot dipped the aircraft's wings for a skimming flight over the restless surface of the sea.

Dozens of vessels – tiny fishing boats, motor launches, yachts and larger cargo ships and tankers – criss-crossed the waves, searching.

On land, the grim hunt for possible survivors continued. Scores of Spanish Guardia Civil, armed with pistols and some with tommy guns slung casually over their shoulders, had been rushed to Palomares. They ordered the bewildered village women and children not to venture into the fields. The men, their bronzed faces grimed black by the smoke and dust, trooped wearily back from their rescue work in twos and threes, too exhausted even to talk.

All the fires had been extinguished. Only thin columns and wisps of smoke now curled from darkened patches of the lush greenery. There was a stillness of death in the air. Even the birds had stopped singing, fluttering from bush to bush in frightened silence. The sun had shrunk behind a bank of grey clouds. Everywhere there was an uneasy calm.

Inside the candle-lit church, Father Navarete offered prayers of thankfulness for 'the miracle that saved Palomares and its people.'

So it was to this bizarre scene that the 'Americanos' finally arrived late that evening. General Wilson, accompanied by Major General Stanley 'Moose' Donavan, Chief of the U.S. Military Mission in Spain, came by car after a 55-mile drive from the airbase nearest to the crash area at Alcantarilla, a few miles from Murcia. The advance task force of 100 airmen, including scientists, technicians and crash experts, had flown in aboard two transport planes from Torregon. They were immediately whisked off to Palomares in military buses along with tons of equipment.

A temporary operations headquarters was soon set up in the middle of a tomato field. Airmen busily erected a tiny tent town while food supplies were unloaded from a convoy truck.

There was barely time for more than a brief preliminary investigation before nightfall. But it indicated to General Wilson that portions of the aircraft debris had almost certainly plunged into the sea.

He reported his findings to the Commander-in-Chief of the U.S. Naval Forces Europe who, in turn, advised the Commander of the Sixth Fleet. It was decided to send a ship to the vicinity as soon as possible. The skipper of the U.S.S. Kiowa (ATF-72), a fleet tug assigned to the Sixth Fleet, was radioed instructions and set course for Palomares.

By darkness the men were encamped and prepared for a 6 a.m. reveille the following day. The senior officers sought out the comforts of every available boarding house, pension, hotel and other lodgings in the area.

Back in Madrid, American ambassador Duke conferred with top Spanish Foreign Ministry officials before authorising a statement giving just the bare facts of the crash.

Tuesday, January 18, dawned dull and grey. Some strange discoveries were to be made that day by the villagers of Palomares. They were to witness some weird search activities, too.

More Spanish civil guards arrived followed by more Air Force personnel. Their first task was to cordon off an area of three square miles in the fields where the tomatoes were shortly due to be picked. This was declared a 'restricted zone'.

The airmen could be observed scouring the fields while carrying eight-foot long bamboo poles and other strange objects. Frequently they stopped to bang into the dry, crusty ground, long sticks from which fluttered triangular red flags.

The men, in khaki fatigues and muddy combat boots, spread out in lines shoulder to shoulder to make sweeping searches. They crawled through canefields and rows of tomato plants, string beans and onions. They beat the bush and tall grass with their poles. And the officers used field telephones to keep in contact with General Wilson at his makeshift operations headquarters.

Pedro Ramirez and all the other worried farmers had meanwhile been given a warning: 'Stay out of the fields. Entry is strictly prohibited.' They were given no explanations. They could only watch, and wonder, and feel a nagging sense of fear.

The search was soon being extended towards the neighbouring villages of Cuevas de Almanzora and Villaricos. The red flags seemed to be sprouting up everywhere. There were white flags, too, and a bigger orange pennant was flying from a crude flagstaff by the deserted Moorish fort near the beach. What did it all mean?

It was now becoming increasingly obvious to the villagers that this was no ordinary air disaster. And the people of Palomares, who for centuries had lived a sheltered existence from the modern world and who in ten terrible minutes had come face to face with the horrors of the Space Age, were afraid.

When they asked what the airmen were searching for they were told simply: 'Parts of the planes.'

The hunt extended to the village itself. Men probed around

the wreckage of a wing section which had fallen near the school. Mangled lumps of metal were dragged away to temporary dumps. Some volunteers toiled up the shingle slope of the mountain range rising up from Villaricos.

A helicopter hovered overhead, its rotor blades scything noisily through the air. The blue and white spotter plane still buzzed back and forth over the fields and was joined by an FA-16 amphibious search plane which swooped down to check positions and locate missing materials.

All that General Wilson was prepared to disclose was that the planes were involved in preliminary work for 'the most difficult task we have to do.'

'The hardest job is still left,' he said. 'The entire area must be mapped out to determine the exact place of each part of the wreckage.'

The single-engine 2-U dived within 100 feet of the General, who stood in his Air Force blue great-coat by a field transmitter which was relaying progress reports on the search. The plane dropped a small red parachute swinging a mysterious black cylinder beneath.

'There is some information that the general is unable to disclose over the transmitting facilities and this is one of the ways he receives a communication,' explained Colonel Young.

A group of five airmen rushed 50 yards to retrieve the vital parcel. The general opened it and laid out large strips of aerial photographs taken of the search area. He and his experts examined the pieces that slowly were beginning to form a huge map of the 'restricted zone.'

So it went on all day with only a brief break for a lunch of hamburgers, onions, chips – and tomatoes!

At 5.30 p.m. the tug Kiowa arrived offshore and commenced a surface reconnaissance.

Then came the grim news that the bodies of the three missing airmen – Sergeant Snyder, the B-52's gunner, and Captain Lane and Captain Simmons, the KC-135's co-pilot and navigator – had been found.

It brought the final death toll of the collision to seven: three crewmen of the bomber and the four-man crew of the tanker.

The number of airmen involved in the strange hunt had, by the evening, swollen to almost 300. More tents were being put up and more provisions were being flown in by helicopters running a shuttle service to and from the Spanish Air Academy at San Javier, almost 90 miles north along the coast past Cartagena.

Still Colonel Young and his aides remained tight-lipped about whether the B-52 had been carrying a nuclear warhead, although one Guardia Civil officer did say in a moment of rare disclosure: 'The Americans have found something, but they are looking for something else. I don't know if what they are looking for is a bomb. They have not told us what they are searching for.'

Air Force engineers were reeling out thousands of yards of cable to establish a phone link from Palomares, via the telephone exchange at nearby Vera, direct to Torrejon airbase.

What General Wilson reported that night did nothing to lessen the consternation among American service chiefs both in Spain and in the Pentagon. A special four-man S.A.C. investigation team was despatched from Washington to Palomares.

* * *

By Wednesday, January 19, newspapers throughout the world were pointing out that a B-52 nuclear bomber might naturally be presumed to be carrying a nuclear bomb.

In Washington, the embarrassed Defence Department declined to comment on the U.P.I. despatch from Palomares that a massive search was underway for a possibly missing nuclear device.

At Torrejon, the U.S. 16th Air Force stayed silent.

The Spanish Press – not scheduled to unlock the shackles of 28 years of censorship for another two months – obediently avoided all mention of the dramatic aftermath of the crash. The State-run radio and television networks confined their reports to the actual crash. So, apart from a brief communiqué from the Spanish Air Ministry three days after the incident referring to a search for 'military secrets', some 30 million Spaniards were mostly kept in the dark. Later, some Spanish newspaper editors did go so far as to harangue the foreign Press for painting a picture of panic and confusion. One paper, in assuring there was no danger, lashed out and said a policeman's ankle sprained during the search hardly constituted 'police casualties.'

The crash could not have occurred at a more disastrous time

and place for Spain. This was the eve of an expected boom year for Spanish tourism. The country was gleefully preparing for an invasion by more than 15 million holidaymakers, among them one million Britons who alone would probably spend an economy-boosting £50 million. Now, an unwanted spotlight was glaring down on this north western outpost of the Costa del Sol. No one could really blame the Spanish government for feeling alarmed and attempting to hush up the strange goings-on at Palomares.

At first light that Wednesday, the airmen, reinforced by several G.I.s, stepped up the hunt. It now seemed obvious that what they were searching for was, indeed, a nuclear bomb. Nobody dared admit that, however.

But the villagers had soon realised that the strange objects they had seen the airmen holding close to the ground were geiger counters for detecting radioactivity.

Many of the officers wore small, square metal badges over their left breast pockets. The badges had no distinguishing names, just a small plastic window with a piece of white paper inside marked with black dots. They were in fact, radiation detectors.

For the 1,200 local inhabitants it was an appalling situation. Already there were alarming stories circulating of a lost atomic bomb lying somewhere outside their backdoors, with no one to refute the stories at this stage, let alone admit that a nuclear warhead was even missing! No wonder many of the villagers were scared out of their wits.

Suppose it was true that there was a missing bomb? Would it explode? Was there danger of contamination? None of the local people really understood about radiation poisoning, and the affects of plutonium or uranium on the human body. Some remembered reading how it could cause cancer and was a deadly bone destroyer.

Fears heightened when it was learned that one of the civil guards had just been rushed to hospital after merely touching some part of the wreckage he had been guarding.

What little information that was forthcoming came not from the Americans, but from the Spaniards. One of the Guardia Civil officers revealed: 'There has been an evacuation of the immediate crash area. All I know is that something important is still missing. There are about 50 or 60 civil guards posted in the area while the Americans search.

'The crash area is closed off so civilians cannot pass through it. I think the bomber fell on the land, but there are some who say it might have fallen in the sea. Anyway, some of the wreckage is on land, and the closest wreckage to the sea is about 500 to 600 metres from the shore.

'I also know that one of our guards has been taken to hospital for observation after touching something. He has no visible injury.'

Colonel Young staunchly kept up his inexhaustible supply of 'No comments.'

When asked what the geiger counters were being used for he replied testily: 'What do you normally use geiger counters for?'

He sternly pointed out that Air Force police, some of them armed with .45 pistols, had been assigned to watch over each piece of the scattered wreckage of the two planes. 'They have been ordered to keep people away.'

Meanwhile, General Wilson, after conferring with the skipper of the Kiowa, realised the limitations of the fleet tug in continuing a sea hunt, as all floating wreckage had been picked up. So he ordered the release of the Kiowa, but as it steamed away he radioed the Commander, Sixth Fleet, to send replacement ships. The minesweepers U.S.S. Sagacity (MSO-469) and U.S.S. Pinnacle (MSO-462), equipped with sonar sounding equipment designed for hunting underwater mines and detecting objects on the ocean floor, were ordered to depart from Barcelona for Palomares.

The four survivors had, by this time, been transferred from the clinics at Aguilas and Vera and flown to the base hospital at Torrejon. There, Captain Wendorf and his three surviving crew were held incommunicado. They were quizzed by the four-man S.A.C. team, from Washington, trying to establish the cause of the crash. Later, after the arrival back from the scene of General Donovan, who gave a briefing for the investigators, they set off to Palomares for an on-the-spot probe.

A team of doctors was also being despatched from Madrid to the area by the Junta de Energia Nuclear – the Spanish Nuclear Energy Commission.

*　　*　　*

Not until the third day did the US Air Force finally break its silence. Mounting speculation and suspicion forced the Americans into making certain revelations.

The bombshell news – later to reverberate round the world and to expose the United States to ridicule and repeated verbal attacks from the Russians and Eastern bloc countries – was contained in a terse, 47-word communiqué issued shortly after 1 p.m. on Thursday, January 20, at Torrejon.

It declared: 'The S.A.C. bomber which was engaged in a refuelling operation off the coast of Spain and suffered an accident with a KC-135 was carrying unarmed nuclear armament. Radiological surveys have established that there is no danger to public health or safety as a result of this accident.'

It was a clear admission that a nuclear weapon had plunged down on Spain or in the Mediterranean either with or from the blazing B-52.

The fate of the weapon was not clarified by Air Force chiefs, who then went back into hiding in their shells of silence. They would not even disclose what exactly the 'nuclear armament' was ... whether it was a missile ... an atomic device ... or a hydrogen bomb. And they refused to say whether the armament had been found or was lost.

The fact that it was 'unarmed' indicated it had not detonated on impact, an explosion which would have blown up the Costa del Sol and its holiday beaches in a mushroom cloud.

Certainly, however, it was the first time that a nuclear weapon had fallen in Europe. How utterly incredible that not a single person on the ground had even been scratched!

Further evaluation of the communiqué soon revealed that following the crash, General Wilson had put into operation a special technique for dealing with accidents involving nuclear armaments. Its code name: 'Broken Arrow'.

A 'Broken Arrow' alert was flashed out whenever a nuclear weapon aboard a plane, warship or armoured vehicle was involved in an accident. Each S.A.C. base had a unit specifically trained in disarming atomic or hydrogen bombs.

Air Force scientists of the Torrejon unit had obviously accompanied General Wilson to Palomares. A backing unit had also been rushed out from America explaining the presence of the four investigators from Washington. But three disturbing questions remained.

Had the experts located the weapon and rendered it harmless? 'No comment!'

Was there more than one weapon involved as the reference to 'nuclear armament' was far from clear? 'No comment!'

And was there the slightest possibility of a nuclear explosion if the weapon was, in fact, lost? 'No comment!'

Strategic Air Command had previously issued diagrams of its basic weapons to emphasise that it was impossible to set off a nuclear explosion by accident because the amount of fissionable material in the bomb was not 'a critical mass' when being transported.

On a B-52, a special arming device was carried, separate from the bomb, which under combat conditions, was inserted in the weapon before it was dropped.

But both hydrogen and atomic bombs contained a fairly substantial quantity of ordinary TNT explosive. This could be set off by an accident, as in the case of a non-nuclear bomb. The resulting explosion would not be nuclear in nature, and could not explode the nuclear material. So it was said. And it was true that a study of official U.S. Air Force records revealed that the crash at Palomares was the thirteenth known American plane accident, involving nuclear devices, without a serious explosion.

The first was on January 13, 1958, when the Air Force said that one of its aircraft had crashed while carrying a nuclear weapon. The Air Force did not reveal where or when the crash occurred, although it was understood to have happened in the United States.

In addition, the following accidents were confirmed:

February 3, 1958 – Hunter Air Force Base, Savannah, Georgia: 'A B-47, following a mid-air collision, jettisoned a portion of a nuclear weapon. The weapon was in transportable configuration and not capable of a nuclear explosion.'

March 1, 1958 – Also from Hunter Air Force Base: 'A B-47, on a routine training flight, accidentally jettisoned an unarmed nuclear weapon, due to a mechanical malfunctioning of the plane's bomb lock system.'

November 4, 1958 – Dyers Air Force Base, Abilene, Texas: 'A B-47 on a routine training mission crashed after take-off. The aircraft carried a nuclear weapon. No atomic explosion and no danger of an atomic explosion. No harmful contamination resulted from the crash.'

November 26, 1958 – Chennault Air Force Base, Iowa : 'A B-47, loaded with a nuclear bomb, caught fire and burned while parked on the flight line. There was no danger of a nuclear explosion and no harmful radiation present.'

July 6, 1959 – Barkdale Air Force Base, Shreveport, Louisiana: 'A C-124 transporting unarmed nuclear weapons crashed and burned on take-off. No explosion and no danger of radiation.'

October 15, 1959 – Glen Bean, Kentucky: 'A B-52 carrying two unarmed nuclear weapons, was involved in a collision with a KC-135, both weapons were found intact and undamaged.'

January 24, 1961 – Seymour Johnson Air Force Base, Goldsboro, North Carolina (the same base from which Captain Wendorf and his six-man crew took off in their ill-fated B-52): 'A B-52 carrying unarmed nuclear weapons crashed 15 miles north of the base.' (The Air Force is, apparently, 'looking' for a bomb still missing over five years after the accident).

March 14, 1961 – Beale Air Force Base, Marysville, California: 'A B-52 carrying an unarmed nuclear weapon crashed. The aircraft was on an airborne alert training flight.'

January 13, 1964 – Turner Air Force Base, Albany, Georgia: 'A B-52 carrying two unarmed nuclear weapons crashed near Cumberland, Maryland. The aircraft was returning from an airborne alert training mission. No danger of nuclear explosion.'

December 8, 1965 – Bunker Hill Air Force Base, Peru, Indiana: 'A B-58 carrying an unarmed nuclear weapon caught fire and burned while moving on a ramp. No danger of an explosion and no harmful radiation present.'

August 19, 1965 – Little Rock Air Force Base, Little Rock, Arkansas: 'A Titan II missile burned in its silo, killing 53 civilian workers. The nuclear warhead had been de-activated and removed before construction work began.'

Apart from the above, the Air Force lists another accident involving a C-124 plane which caught fire and burned at Wright-Patterson Air Force Base, Dayton, Ohio, on October 12, 1965. However, the report states: 'Nuclear weapons not carried – just non-explosive components of nuclear systems.'

This remarkable document of disasters was climaxed by the

accident at Palomares. And back in the barren coastal area, where now over 400 men were engaged in the search, more startling developments were taking place.

Around General Wilson's field headquarters a unit of Guardia Civil stood impassively on the alert. Their smart olive uniforms and shiny tricorn helmets contrasted sharply with the airmen and G.I.s, many of them unshaven, in their fatigues and muddy boots.

In addition to the geiger counters, it was noticed that officers were now carrying other specialised electronic equipment. One strange object was rather like a telephone receiver. It was pressed to the ground while a reading was taken on a dial on the large aluminium box to which is was attached by a coiled wire. This, it was later discovered, was an alpha scintillation meter, a counter used for detecting deadly alpha rays, the fast-moving helium nucleus ejected by some radioactive atoms.

Palomares, so it seemed, was contaminated.

CHAPTER THREE

ROBERTO PUIG was curious. Everyone for miles around was talking apprehensively about the air disaster. And the more he listened, the more curious he became. So Senor Puig, the municipal architect of Mojacar, decided to drive to Palomares and have a look around.

He had no business commitments that morning. What could be more pleasant than to motor along the winding coastal road, and then stroll down to the sandy beach? The sun was shining, and the temperature, although it was only January, was in the mid-seventies.

Senor Puig, stocky and balding, deeply inhaled the fresh salty air with its tang of seaweed. There were no Americans or Spanish police in sight but he could see dozens of tiny figures in the distance combing through the fields by Palomares.

He decided not to venture too near the village as he knew he would only be turned back. So he plodded along the beach and round the headland. About half a mile ahead was the outline of the old Moorish fort, perched on a tiny cliff by the dried-up Almanzora riverbed.

Senor Puig spotted a lump of mangled plane wreckage which had been washed up on the shore. He went over to investigate. It appeared to be part of a wing, but he could not be sure. He dragged it up on to the beach, leaving it prominently displayed for the Americans to collect later.

He walked on slowly and as he neared the fort noticed several men talking earnestly together. The architect took a winding footpath up the cliffside and soon found himself less than 100 yards from the fort.

It was then that his gaze was attracted by a strange object embedded in the dark brown soil and which was glinting in the sunlight.

He had no idea what it might be and walked across to take a closer look. He saw the object must have ploughed into the

44

bone-dry ground with considerable force as it had made a largish, egg-shaped crater.

Senor Puig knelt down to peer inside. To his horror he realised he was face to face with a bomb.

Sweat glistened on his forehead and his first reaction was one of incredible surprise. His next reaction was one of fear. For all he knew the bomb could explode at any minute. He wanted to get out of the area as quickly as possible.

He clutched at the edge of the crater, intending to stand up, but at that precise moment felt an unaccustomed, tingling sensation above his left knee. It was not all that painful but when he looked at the knee he saw that a red burn, slightly smaller than a sixpence, had suddenly appeared on his flesh.

By now Senor Puig was a frightened man indeed.

Then he heard a shout from the distance. 'Fuera! Vayase!' He turned to see a Spanish Guardia Civil running towards him, frantically waving his arms. 'Get out of this area immediately!'

The architect did not linger to argue. Rubbing the tiny, still tingling burn on his knee he departed along the beach.

Later, the news of his burn and his encounter with the bomb, spread through the area. He was 'taken-in' at the request of the Americans and examined by a doctor.

He related afterwards: 'There had been no Civil guard patrolling the place and I walked up to the crater not thinking for a minute that there might be a bomb in it. In my wildest dreams I never imagined that there could be a nuclear weapon near the beach.

'It was stuck in the ground, pointing upwards with about three feet of it exposed. It was round – just like an oversized bullet – and about a foot and a half wide. A bronze cylindrical peg about three inches in diameter was attached to the nose.

'There was a one-inch thick band, olive-drab in colour, around the silver cylinder and it had white lettering on it. I could not understand the words because they were in English. The bomb was tilted at an angle of about 45 degrees.

'It was a shock experience. I think it is intolerable that the Spanish Government allows these nuclear-armed planes to fly over our territory and thus endanger Spanish lives and property. It is a danger to world peace.'

Senor Puig suffered no apparent ill-effects from his encounter with the nuclear bomb and eventually the burn disappeared from his knee. However, for a considerable time afterwards he was the object of intense study by both American and Spanish scientists and doctors.

Senor Puig's sortie of fear cleared up one of the mysteries. The 'nuclear armament' was definitely a bomb.

The story of his encounter circulated among the local populus and the horrors of it grew in proportion as his story was told and retold. And fears for their safety intensified in the minds of the simple, innocent local people.

Their concern was even more intensified as frantic hunt operations were carried out by the U.S. Forces. Could it be that more than just one bomb was involved? It looked, ominously, as though this was the case.

*   *   *

In 'Campamento Wilson' – as the growing tent town under the command of General Wilson had now been christened – an impressive array of mechanical equipment was beginning to build up after 48 hours. There were yellow-painted bulldozers fork-lift trucks, water wagons, caterpillar tractors with earth-moving shovels, transport lorries, jeeps and even two ambulances. Strangely, their distinctive red crosses had been blacked out by pasting sheets of brown paper over them. If the idea of this was to conceal their nature, it was a farce!

More unwelcome arrivals were the first inquisitive Press men on the scene – Leo White, bespectacled, Manchester-based reporter for the London *Daily Mirror,* who had been switched from another assignment in Madrid to Palomares, and Andre del Amo, a 24-year-old, fluent Spanish-speaking American from the Madrid bureau of United Press International. After their all-night, 365-mile drive from the Spanish capital, both initially encountered the non-stop battery of 'No comment' answers to their questions from Colonel Young. But their subsequent talks with the villagers, coupled with what they observed and discovered in the tomato fields, provided a world 'scoop'.

No one barred them entry from the restricted zone. They strolled unchallenged along dusty footpaths bordering the fields and inspected lumps of charred wreckage, until a burly American

Air Force police sergeant spotted the two journalists and raced across.

'Hey, you guys! You'd better get outta this area! It's contaminated!' he yelled.

The sergeant pointed to a nearby heap of twisted, silver-coloured metal and said: 'I wouldn't go near that because it's very likely to be one of the sources of radiation contamination in this area. It could even be part of the missing bomb.'

White and del Amo backed-off hurridly and then produced their Press credentials to explain their presence. The sergeant seemed satisfied.

'Look fellas, I've got a problem,' the sergeant went on. 'Do either of you speak Spanish by any chance? There's an obstinate old farmer over there who just can't understand that I'm trying to instruct him to leave his field. Could you come over with me and tell him he must get out of the field immediately because of the radiation danger?'

Del Amo walked across to the bean field where the farmer, sun-burned and wearing a black beret, was working. He was obviously annoyed at being disturbed and continued to cut beans with his sickle while his long-eared donkey looked on impassively. 'I know nothing about radiation,' said the old man with an almost bored expression. 'I am cutting my beans to feed my mule and I must also take some home for my family.' Only when he had collected sufficient beans did the farmer reluctantly shuffle off towards Palomares, muttering angrily to himself. The sergeant, hands on hips, breathed a sigh of relief.

'How is the search progressing?' ventured the two reporters, casually.

'Well, there's still one bomb missing,' explained the sergeant without hesitation. 'There are no clues at the moment as to where it might be. It could have fallen near the village and buried itself in the ground on impact, or it might even be in the sea.'

'And the other bombs? What happened to them?' asked the reporters, hoping that their carefully-phrased question would not be noticed by the unsuspecting sergeant, as sheer guess-work on their part.

His frank reply was stunning. 'Two of the bombs, as you probably know, were found within about 18 hours of the crash.'

Then, sweeping the area with his finger he pointed towards

the Moorish fort overlooking the beach about a mile south-east of the field in which they were standing and said: 'The third bomb was found there, practically on the beach.'

White and del Amo could hardly believe their ears. If what the sergeant was saying was correct – and they could see no reason to doubt his word – they were on to the biggest story of their careers, a story of dramatic proportions which, when disclosed to the world, would undoubtedly produce consternation and reactions at the highest levels of international diplomacy.

When the reporters reached Palomares, they found that speculation among the villagers had begun to grow as soon as word spread that a civil guard had been taken to hospital, that Senor Puig was being examined by doctors and that the area could be contaminated. Lack of official information was making them angry.

'We are already scared. Now we are also annoyed because we don't really know the truth about what is happening,' said Senor Francisco Gallardo Lopez, the 48-year-old tobacconist. 'The Americans should tell us what is going on, then perhaps we would not be so frightened. People keep talking about nuclear bombs. What is it all about? What does it mean?'

Schoolteacher Pedro Sanchez, although puzzled, tried to be practical. 'The Americans will have to take care of any contamination that might result from this accident – if there is contamination,' he said.

One villager, an old man known simply as Juanito, walked up to correspondent del Amo and asked: 'How do you say "burro" in English?'

He pointed to a young American airman, second-class, who was standing guard by the wreckage which had fallen near the schoolhouse, and said contemptuously: 'I want to call that Yankee guard a burro (donkey).' In his simplicity he added: 'We don't need him here.'

* * *

Piece by piece, little by little, the shocking truth about the doomed B-52 and its cargo, and what had happened to Palomares, was revealed. It was apparent that not one but four deadly nuclear bombs had fallen out of the sky when the Stratofortress

disintegrated. Three of them had been accounted for – the fourth
was lost.

Eventually, it was to be learned authoritatively although un-
officially, that the bombs were monstrous, 25-megaton devices,
each containing an explosive capacity equivalent to 25,000,000
tons of TNT and 5,000 times more powerful than the atomic
bomb dropped on Hiroshima in 1945.

The world would have been plagued by an unseen, lurking
cloud of radioactive dust if, by a freak chance, one of those bombs
had detonated in the air above Palomares on January 17. Had
all four exploded, American scientists admit the consequences
following such a nuclear blast would have been 'almost beyond
comprehension.'

Everything within an estimated eight miles radius around
Palomares would have been wiped out if just one bomb had gone
off. On land, the neighbouring villages of Villaricos, Vera, Cuevas
de Almanzora, Garrucha, Mojacar and Turre would have been
flattened with not a single survivor. The immediate death toll,
despite the area being sparsely populated, would have been as
high as 50,000. At sea, passing ships and fishing boats, together
with their passengers and crews, would have disintegrated into
nothing.

Within a 50 miles radius shock waves from the mushrooming
holocaust would have caused large-scale damage, scorching the
earth, setting alight all combustible material and spreading fires.
There would have been uncontrollable panic at the many holiday
resorts dotted along the Costa del Sol, including Almeria, the
capital town of the province, and in the mountain villages to the
north-west, including some in the rugged Sierra Nevada range.
Inevitably, casualties would have been high as men, women and
children either inhaled or swallowed invisible alpha particles,
which can cause cancer and bone diseases.

The poisonous radioactive fallout would have been prevalent
within a radius of 400 miles – enveloping practically the entire
Iberian peninsular of Spain and Portugal, northern Algeria and
the cities of Algiers and Oran, a considerable part of Morocco
including Tangier, Rabat, Casablanca and Marrakesh, the Rock
of Gibraltar, and an area of France across the Pyrenees possibly
extending from Biarritz to Toulouse and Perpignan. Additionally,
a strong wind could have blown the fearsome radioactive cloud

right across Europe – France, Italy, Switzerland, Austria, Germany, Belgium, Holland, England, Wales, Ireland or Scotland. Perhaps even beyond the Iron Curtain to Russia!

So much for what might have happened. Why then, did not one of the nuclear bombs explode? There are various reasons, including the nature of atoms themselves, the way a nuclear bomb is built, the safety features incorporated in a bomb, the ingenious and complicated trigger devices, and the safety precautions enforced in handling a bomb.

A Washington scientist explains, in simplified terms, how extremely difficult it is to explode a nuclear bomb, even intentionally, because of the nature of atoms.

'The difficulty stems from the inherent nature of atoms. The heart, or nucleus, of an atom resists being split – splitting is needed for an atomic explosion – with a tenacity unimaginably stronger than any forces known in ordinary experience. The forces are much stronger than any glue, cement, or welding process. The "glue" holding the atomic nucleus together – scientists call them "binding forces" – are the strongest known forces in nature. The splitting of atoms is known as "fission", and an "atomic" bomb is a fission bomb.

'It is even more difficult to explode a hydrogen bomb. It is so difficult it requires a fission bomb to trigger the explosion. The reason is that it is more difficult to unite, or fuse, atoms than it is to split them. In a hydrogen bomb, nuclei of hydrogen atoms are forced to unite, releasing enormous amounts of energy – the blast itself. ɹydrogen bomb is a thermonuclear or fusion bomb.

'After 21 years of developing, testing, storing, transporting, flying, overhauling, modifying, inspecting and otherwise handling nuclear weapons, the United States has never had an accident in which the nuclear component exploded or caused injury and damage.

'Several accidents scattered bomb ingredients such as plutonium, but none were atomic blasts. To understand how hard it is to explode a nuclear weapon, consider how one is built.

'An atomic bomb consists of a shell of ordinary explosives, like TNT, with an inner core of nuclear material. The nuclear material can be uranium 235, plutonium 239, or both. The inner core is the bomb.

'The shell is covered with detonators, like dots on a child's balloon. The detonators, activated by an electric charge from a battery, set off the conventional explosives, which actually squeeze against the nuclear material. This squeezing, or "implosion", compresses the nuclear material so that the atoms come close enough together to sustain a chain reaction. The reaction, sudden and over within a moment, is the atomic explosion.

'However, to achieve the reaction, the detonators must all work together with split-second timing. If the atomic material is not squeezed inwardly, uniformly, no nuclear explosion occurs. If the conventional explosives on one side of the bomb detonate before the explosives on the other side, the nuclear material is merely scattered. Instead of the critical components being brought together, they are separated.

'When plutonium is scattered there is some concern about alpha radiation given off by the material. If alpha particles are inhaled in large quantities in the lungs, or get into the bloodstream through a cut, health may be endangered. However, the number of rays given off from a bomb's scattering is small and below the permissible dose permitted to workers in atomic plants. Alpha particles can travel only an inch and can be stopped by a sheet of paper or the outer layer of skin.

'To build more safety into nuclear bombs, various things are done. For example, bombs are carried in flight "unarmed" or "defused". This means that wires are not connected to detonators; or switches to activate the detonators are locked in the off position; or trigger and bomb are physically separated. An arming device – trigger – may be located so that it takes a series of switches, thrown in the proper sequence, to make it operable.

'Even in the event of nuclear war and purposeful dropping of nuclear bombs, the weapons would not detonate unless an intricate series of events had been satisfied.

'To ensure that bombs are as accident proof as it is humanly possible, the Atomic Energy Commission – which makes U.S. nuclear weapons – is continually subjecting them to "torture" tests. Unarmed bombs have been dropped from aeroplanes. The A.E.C. has put an atomic weapon on a rocket sled, sped it down a rail track at more than 1,500 miles an hour and slammed it into a thick concrete wall. In another test, the weapon was set on fire in a pool of flaming oil. In no case did the nuclear material in the weapon explode, although the conventional explosives, in some cases, did.'

However, had the people of Palomares and thereabouts been told all this it would have given them little comfort, even if they had been able to understand it all. For they knew only that something extremely dangerous and unusual had happened. And they were scared stiff.

*   *   *

By 2 p.m. on Friday, January 21, the two minesweepers, U.S.S. Sagacity and U.S.S. Pinnacle, had arrived off the coast of Palomares from Barcelona.

They immediately began sweeping the area with their underwater electronic mine detection equipment and their 'hard hat' divers – men wearing diving suits – began searching the offshore waters to a depth of approximately 60 feet.

These two minesweepers were soon joined by U.S.S. Skill (MSO-471) and U.S.S. Nimble (MSO-468), both attached to the Navy's Mine Division Eighty-four.

With the increased naval activity and the grey outline of the ships silhouetted against the horizon, the possibility of the lost nuclear bomb lying on the Mediterranean seabed became more apparent.

Incredibly, fact was taking on the fictional undertones of a James Bond thriller. The creator of Bond, the late Ian Fleming, would himself have been amazed at the similarities of the Palomares incident to his ninth '007' escapade 'Thunderball', in which two hi-jacked atomic bombs are held for £100 million ransom under the sea after super-criminals had deliberately crashed a nuclear bomber in the ocean off the Bahama Islands.

Well, here, off-shore from Palomares, was probably a missing atomic bomb. There was even a man named Bond in the thick of the recovery operation. Admittedly, not James Bond, but Robert E. Bond, a U.S. Navy frogman from Louisville, Kentucky!

And although there was no sign of any SPECTRE agents trying to steal the bomb from under the noses of the Americans, Russia was already taking more than just a casual interest in the incident!

'Thunderball'? perhaps it would be more appropriate in this

instance to substitute 'Thunderboob'?

Ashore, General Wilson decided to move his tent-town head-quarters out of the tomato field to a more permanent position near the beach, where he could maintain easier contact by flash-ing coded messages to the growing flotilla of ships. In any case, the land force had now increased to 450 men and there was hardly room to put up any more clusters of tents among the tomatoes.

The bulldozers were soon at work, levelling off the sand dunes on the site of the new encampment and transforming the bumpy, rutted cart-tracks into something more resembling roads so that the steady stream of large and small military vehicles could be driven almost on to the beach.

Throughout the daylight hours the men, shoulder to shoulder and carrying geiger counters and other electronic equipment, still continued their relentless hunt in the Spanish 'badlands', so-called because of the region's generally sparse and sun-dried vegetation.

And still the official U.S. silence persisted. 'Is it true that a nuclear bomb has been lost?' Colonel Young was asked.

'I don't know anything about a missing bomb,' he insisted, with a shrug of the shoulders.

'Well, what is everyone searching for?'

'Oh, just wreckage of the planes,' was his bland, unconvincing reply.

'Have three bombs already been found?'

'I have no information about that!'

'What information do you have then?'

'None!'

Understandably, the villagers felt hostility and bitterness at the intrusion of the Americans with their secretive attitude. As a search party spread out across the tomato patch where he had been digging, a peasant wiped his brow and muttered: 'Why don't they collect their ashes and go?'

Only minor details of the official Air Force admission that one of the planes in the multi-million pound crash had been carrying unarmed nuclear armament were beginning to filter back to Palomares. There were the continued fears of radioactivity after several farmers had been warned to get out of their fields as they were working in a contaminated area.

The acting mayor, Senor Jose Manuel Gonzalez, said: 'It is all very bewildering. Just now I have been advised that the villagers should not drink the milk from local cows or goats and that they should not eat chickens, eggs or home-grown vegetables because of the possible danger of contamination.

'Food supplies will have to be brought to Palomares. I am afraid this bad news will do nothing to calm the general fears. We are country folk used to a simple, carefree life. All this talk of radiation is beyond the comprehension of some of the villagers. They just don't realise the seriousness of the situation.'

Scientists of the Junta de Energia Nuclear, with the initials J.E.N. stitched in bold blue on the breast pockets of their white medical coats, had begun to arrive. They prepared a makeshift surgery and consulting room in the small village cinema.

The Commission's President and Director General, Senor Jose Otero de Navascues, announced plans for everyone to undergo compulsory tests for radioactivity.

At Cuevas de Almanzora a spokesman in the town hall summed it all up by saying: 'Everyone is frightened to death about what is happening. The prospect of possibly having a nuclear bomb outside our back doors is not very pleasant. I am told that three bombs have been found and they are still searching. I suppose there must be more.'

*　　*　　*

Back in Madrid, the recently-appointed U.S. ambassador to Spain, 49-year-old Mr Angier Biddle Duke, after less than a fortnight in his new job, found himself in the thick of a diplomatic crisis. To say the least, the Spanish government was highly displeased at having nuclear bombs raining down and endangering the lucrative tourist trade near the sunshine beaches.

It was a situation in which skilled diplomacy would be vitally necessary if smooth, friendly relations between America and Spain were to be maintained.

Mr Duke had the necessary qualifications to fulfil this role. His previous post had been that of Chief of Protocol for the administrations of both assassinated President John F. Kennedy and President Lyndon B. Johnson. During World War II he had served with the Air Force and under War Secretary Stimson.

Then followed various posts with the diplomatic corps in Buenos Aires and Madrid before his 1952 appointment by President Harry S. Truman as ambassador to tiny El Salvador. He was then the youngest envoy in U.S. history. Fifteen months later he resigned to join the International Rescue Committee, an organisation of which he eventually became president, and visited world trouble spots like Vietnam, in 1955, to study the refugee problem, Berlin, 1956, to check on Soviet repatriation practices, and the Austro-Hungarian border that same year to supervise treatment of refugees from the revolution.

He boosted the vote for his long-time friend John Kennedy in the 1960 presidential election by his campaigning for the Democrats in Latin America. After victory, Kennedy selected him for the White House protocol post in January, 1961, a task in which he was called upon to entertain countless visiting Royalty, statesmen and government leaders. 'It's a great satisfaction to have been as close as I have to the sources of the world's power,' he once said.

Now, in Madrid, he realised that once the Spaniards learned that American warplanes with nuclear arms aboard were flying over Spanish territory, there could be serious trouble.

The Spanish government was still clamping a complete blackout throughout the country on news revealing that it was a nuclear bomber involved in the crash.

But word was already spreading, despite the ban. University students and intellectuals, for example, were able to read detailed reports in foreign newspapers openly displayed and on sale at the many news-stands. Short wave news bulletins from other European countries also included extensive coverage, although not a word of the Palomares incident was being broadcast in the hourly news-casts from Torrejon airbase on its Spain-Morocco FM network.

The ambassador was seriously concerned that a rash of anti-American demonstrations might erupt which could jeopardise the U.S.-Spanish agreement granting America permission to maintain the three S.A.C. bases in Spain, as well as the Polaris submarine headquarters.

Attention could not have been directed towards Palomares at a more unfortunate time. Relations between the two countries were at their cordial highest. During a recent stop-over in

Madrid, Secretary of State Dean Rusk had been warmly received by top government officials and it was apparent that Franco and other Spanish leaders voiced complete sympathy with the U.S. position in Vietnam.

Now, some incensed Spaniards were already voicing stern criticism of the government policy allowing U.S. nuclear bombers to fly over Spanish territory. Among them was Senor Puig, the architect who saw one of the bombs. Referring to Spain's bitter struggle for the return of the Rock of Gibraltar after 262 years of British rule, he said: 'It is a paradox that Spain worries so much about Gibraltar when the U.S. bases on Spanish territory constitute a much greater danger.'

Leading lawyer Senor Manuel Fuentes commented: 'Planes carrying nuclear bombs should be equipped with the best possible security systems to avoid any chance of disaster. We are not at war to be endangered every minute of the day by those planes flying over Spain.'

'I think such dangerous devices should not be flying over us for any reason,' said Madrid engineer, Senor Francisco Gomez. 'They could cause tragedy some day.'

Later, the villagers of Palomares, when they understood more what it was all about, expressed bitterness over their plight and generally agreed it was just plain 'tonteria' – foolishness – for nuclear bombers to fly over Spanish soil.

But there were those who differed. Senor Francisco Haro, 36, owner of the hilltop Hotel Indalo in Mojacar reasoned: 'I think it is far more dangerous to give Russia the edge in the cold war than to consider the possibility of a freak accident that would involve four or five lives or even a few hundred.'

Top Spanish journalist, Senor Jose Gonzalez said: 'I agree with those who think such flights should be safe enough to rule out the smallest chance of explosion or radio activity. But, on the other hand, the flights should not be halted. It is the price the West seems obliged to pay because of the cold war.'

The issue, however, was soon to extend to other European countries. *The disaster at Palomares was to indicate vividly the fact that the same kind of accident could occur again in England... or France... or Holland... or West Germany... or, of course, anywhere and at any time along the routes where the nuclear bombers still patrol the skies.*

Certainly, Spain was far from oblivious to the political and military risks involved. And four days after the crash – on January 21 – the government posed the crash as 'evidence of the dangers created by N.A.T.O.'s use of the Gibraltar airstrip.'

Franco announced a prohibition on all military aircraft of the North Atlantic Treaty Organisation from flying over Spanish territory to and from Gibraltar. It meant that the aircraft would be forced to make huge detours around Spanish air corridors. But the government stressed that the ban was not directed in any way against the member countries of N.A.T.O. It was more of a reprisal against Gibraltar in the continued quarrel with Britain over the future of the Rock. Indeed, a decree warned that Spain would no longer consider Gibraltar as a N.A.T.O. base, and would not in any way facilitate its use as such.

Pierre Brisard, the genial giant – 6′ 3″ tall – among Madrid newsmen, and Director in Spain of Agence France Presse, explained the government's move, in a despatch to Paris, as resulting from the heavy risks weighing on Spain from Gibraltar's use as a N.A.T.O. base, risks from which Spain failed to benefit. The Gibraltar situation had forced Spain to cope with two opposing military alliances – N.A.T.O. and the Warsaw Pact. The Russians, speaking on the one side, had warned in the United Nations that they considered Gibraltar a N.A.T.O. military fortress, with the consequences that implied for Spain.

Warning of the aerial blockade had, in any case, been hinted at over a month earlier, when Foreign Minister Castiella had told the Spanish Cortes – parliament – in a major policy speech, that Spain could not consider Gibraltar as a military base for N.A.T.O.

The crash of the nuclear bomber helped only to strengthen the Spanish case and serve as an example of the risks involved in extending N.A.T.O.'s fly-over rights.

So Franco was no longer prepared to take all the consequences and none of the benefits in the case of Gibraltar and N.A.T.O., although, at this stage, he was apparently prepared to accept the risk of U.S. nuclear overflights, bearing in mind the fruitful military pact. The initial reaction of N.A.T.O. countries at the flight ban was one of annoyance for being drawn into the Anglo-Spanish dispute over Gibraltar.

Most military aircraft of N.A.T.O. countries used Gibraltar as a standard refuelling stop on flights to Africa. The ban on the Rock necessitated, for aircraft, what was described sourly by the air attaché of an embassy whose country was a N.A.T.O. member, as 'an annoying and irksome detour.' The ban did not, of course, affect Britain, the one N.A.T.O. country using the Rock more than any other, because Spain recognised the British *legal* right to have a base there. An average of two R.A.F. planes a day flew and continued to fly over Spain, back and forth from Gibraltar to England.

Nor did the no-trespassing decision really affect the United States although their N.A.T.O. planes were supposedly included in the ban. The presence of the Strategic Air Command bases throughout the country provided an escape route for continued U.S. air activity.

* * *

The crash of the B-52, despite its more serious implications, was providing some light relief in the form of dry Spanish jokes. The coast around Palomares was now being affectionately referred to as the 'Costa Boom' and the 'Costa Bomba'.

There was the true story of the fisherman ejected from a distant bar because he told the owner he had just visited Palomares and everyone was convinced he was radio active.

Madrilenians, sweltering in the sun, talked with relief of the Spanish capital becoming a coastal resort.

Jokes of atomic beans on sale in the markets were becoming stale. But, still managing to raise a laugh, was the suggestion that the farmers of Palomares had stopped growing tomatoes in favour of mushrooms– big ones!

* * *

By Saturday, January 22, operation 'Broken Arrow' showed no signs of a let up. The feverish activity at 'Campamento Wilson' continued unabated.

More and more troops were arriving by the hour. Nearly 600 men were now engaged in the vast hunt of an area extending beyond the tomato fields of Palomares, along the dried-up and wreckage-littered Almanzora riverbed, towards, Vera, Villaricos and the hamlet of La Hoya del Algarrobo.

'We are looking for anything. Those are our instructions,' said one officer leading a group of 150 fatigue-clad airmen.

More tons of equipment was also being brought into the camp including generators, four huge refrigerators, mobile laundry machines and even a projector for an outdoor cinema.

Further findings by the Air Force using its spotter and reconnaissance planes indicated to General Wilson that a considerable amount of wreckage had fallen into the sea. The four minesweepers on the scene confirmed this finding by recording a number of positive contacts through their sonar detecting equipment. Most of the objects located were, however, at considerable depths, beyond the limits of frogmen and the 'hard-hat' divers. Orange coloured buoys were set afloat to mark the spots.

It was becoming clear that Navy reinforcements would certainly be necessary in the recovery of aircraft debris and other mysterious objects on the seabed.

General Wilson, studying a mass of charts, photographs and other data in his low-slung tent office, eventually filed a request for assistance which was flashed through to the Secretary of the Navy shortly after noon on January 22.

*　　*　　*

The weather in Palomares, predictably, was hot. The sun shone from a cloudless sky. The birds were singing again. Pink almond blossom was in full bloom. In the shaded groves the green lemons and oranges were beginning to change colour as they ripened, hanging limp and dusty from the sagging, laden trees.

But in the scorched tomato fields the crops were already beginning to wither in the heat. The promise of a bumper year was rotting away. For within the 600 acres of the restricted zone the crops had been declared 'untouchable' by American and Spanish scientists. To farmers like Pedro Ramirez, Miguel Castro and Jose Portillo it could have meant ruin.

It had been estimated that farmers produced locally a colossal 154,000 to 198,000 pounds of tomatoes daily for shipment to foreign markets. Now they complained of losing thousands of pounds in unfulfilled export shipments. No one, they declared, would buy their products since the crash because of the fear that the tomatoes had been contaminated by radio activity from the nuclear devices.

The U.S. government was faced with no alternative but to promise the farmers 'adequate compensation' for their crop losses. A claims office was opened at the camp, staffed by American and Spanish Air Force personnel. In the meantime, the families of approximately 200 workers temporarily unemployed because of operation 'Broken Arrow' were awarded a daily allowance of 150 pesetas, about 18s.

Outside the ramshackle cinema building at Palomares, a long line of villagers straggled down the cobbled street and around the corner. There were women clutching babies, teenage boys and girls, and men in their muddied farming clothes and black berets, an almost compulsory traditional headgear for the locals which was being fast adopted by the American troops. They talked in hushed whispers, looking nervous and apprehensive.

Some were queueing up to be examined for traces of radio-activity by the teams of doctors from the Spanish Nuclear Energy Commission.

So far no one had been found suffering from a lethal dose of alpha rays but it was no secret that an undisclosed number of Spanish Guardia Civil, on duties around the area where a bull-dozer was digging out what was perhaps a nuclear bomb, had been exposed to radiation. Some of these men had apparently been helping to dig out the object which was deeply embedded in the ground.

The captain of the civil guard freely admitted, when questioned, that he was one of the contamination victims. But he told U.P.I. reporter Tony Navarro: 'I would be in the hospital, not talking to you, if I had suffered severe radiation.'

Inside the somewhat stuffy atmosphere of the emergency clinic, with its distinctive musty cinema odour, one of the doctors explained: 'The slight traces of radioactivity found on these men should completely disappear within about two days. They are not likely to suffer any ill effects.'

But the bewildered villagers were not much comforted when they were next advised to burn any clothing which they had worn in the fields since the day of the crash!

Senor Gonzalez, the acting mayor, urged everyone in

Palomares who might accidentally have touched or handled parts of the widely scattered plane wreckage to submit themselves for medical examination. His appeal spurred the mayors in the surrounding pueblos of Vera, Garrucha and Cuevas de Almanzora to take similar action.

At Palomares alone, 150 people a day filed through the clinic, some even undergoing blood and urine tests.

All this was happening just 48 hours after an American assurance that there was no health hazard to civilians.

More dramatic developments were about to take place. General Wilson, following top-level discussions among military chiefs in Spain and at the Pentagon, prepared to fly back to Madrid on a secret mission.

CHAPTER FOUR

A T THE PORT of Aguilas, Francisco Simo, the fisherman who had witnessed the crash of the B-52, heard of the gigantic American search and of the disturbing rumours of a lost nuclear bomb. A man of good memory, who knew his fishing waters as well as most men know the way they part their hair, Simo was also a man of considerable intelligence.

Crystal clear in his mind remained those dramatic minutes, when the red and white parachutes drifted down from the sky with the survivors; when another parachute splashed into the sea with a light blue box attached, and when the bigger, greyish parachute with the large, strange object dangling from it also, sank not far from his fishing vessel.

'Perhaps this was the big bomb they are supposed to be looking for?' he mused. 'Well, there is no harm in telling them where it fell in the water. I could take them to the exact spot.'

Senor Simo felt a chill of excitement. He would make an official report of what he had seen. He set out immediately for the harbour offices.

*　　*　　*

It was one of those all-too-rare occasions – a day off – and at his home in Naples, Italy, Rear Admiral William S. Guest, United States Navy, was relaxing.

The 52-year-old admiral, Deputy Commander of the Naval Striking and Support Forces, Southern Europe – a N.A.T.O. command – looked forward to spending his Sundays at home with his family. Invariably, there was so much to do it was impossible, but on January 23 it seemed that all was quiet for a change.

It was a warm day and his two sons Robert, aged 14, and Douglas, 11, were playing noisily outside. His wife, Tina, was busily preparing lunch in the kitchen. Guest settled down in a comfortable armchair to catch up on his reading of a pile of old newspapers, for he liked keeping in touch with the news of affairs back home in San Diego, California.

The admiral was so engrossed in one of the papers that, at first, he barely noticed the persistent ringing of the telephone in the hallway. Then, frowning with exasperation, he neatly folded up the copy of the *Los Angeles Times*, walked into the hall, and and picked up the receiver.

His wife inwardly sighed when she heard the phone. Instinctively she knew that her husband was about to be summoned away on another assignment. She hoped she was wrong. Through the open doorway she could hear snatches of his conversation.

'. . . Where did you say? Palomares?'

There was a silence as the caller gave a lengthy explanation.

'. . . considerable wreckage and equipment in the sea, you say? . . . recovery operation off the coast of Spain . . . yes . . . straight away!'

The knuckles of his right hand were white as the admiral tightly gripped the phone, and stared straight ahead, occasionally nodding his head, and listening intently.

'. . . an important briefing . . . yes . . . I understand . . . Torrejon airbase, near Madrid . . . I will make the necessary arrangements immediately.'

Within half-an-hour Admiral Guest was striding briskly from his house to the waiting naval staff car parked outside. He paused briefly to turn and wave a farewell to his wife and two sons standing in the doorway, then climbed into the back seat. The chauffeur deftly manoeuvred the sleek limousine through the hooting traffic, heading in the direction of the military base where an aircraft and crew were already waiting on the tarmac.

The admiral had arranged for the fastest available transportation to take him to Torrejon and two hours after the phone call interruption at his home, he was airborne.

The day before, as soon as General Wilson had filed his request for assistance to the Secretary of the Navy, it had been given top priority. The Chief of Naval Operations had advised the Commander-in-Chief of the U.S. Naval Forces in Europe of the acceptance of his request, and 12 hours later the Commander, Sixth Fleet, had designated Admiral Guest as the on-scene commander for the Navy portion of the aircraft salvage operations. A number of ships were also assigned to take part in the search, under the collective name of Task Force 65.

Admiral Guest was an ideal choice as commander of this task force. During his 30 years of commissioned service he had served in almost every type of naval ship. As a naval aviator for 27 years, he had participated in many operations involved in crash investigations and aircraft salvage. His combat record was brilliant. He had served on assignments during World War II and during the Korean conflict. He was the holder of the Navy Cross, Combat Legion of Merit, Combat Bronze Star, Air Medal, Navy Commendation Medal, Presidential Unit Citation and Navy Unit Citation. His thirteen battle stars represented 13 major battles of World War II and he was the first carrier pilot to sink a Japanese ship after Pearl Harbor.

Only 90 minutes after take-off from Naples the admiral's plane was circling slowly above the mist-shrouded skyscraper buildings of the Spanish capital, preparing to land at Torrejon airbase. A bevy of American military chiefs was already assembling there, including General Wilson and the four crew survivors of the B-52, for a top-secret conference with Guest.

That morning Spain was learning for the first time details of the plane crash, with actual reference to the nuclear armament, which, previously, had been censored.

The Catholic daily newspaper *Ya* revealed in a report that a nuclear device was missing. It said: 'Units of the Spanish and U.S. Navy, with a group of helicopters, are searching the zone near the coast in operations that are being carried out to recover elements of a secret military character, including nuclear armament.'

And the semi-official government news agency, Cifra, claimed that the minesweeper U.S.S. Pinnacle had made sonar contact with two mysterious objects at a depth of some 2,000 feet – approximately 1,700 feet apart – at a distance of about three miles off the coast of Villaricos.

At Torrejon, Major Ernest Moore, who had been left in charge of the Information Office following Colonel Young's departure to Palomares, was bombarded with a barrage of questions. But he gave few answers. He refused to confirm whether two objects had been located on the Mediterranean seabed. He was not prepared to say that the two objects, if they existed, were possibly parts of a missing nuclear device. He could not comment when asked if there was danger of contamination to Spanish coastal waters from nuclear armament in the sea.

And, he insisted, he knew nothing about 'a lost bomb.'

So the question and no-answer farce went on, only serving to cause the United States harm and embarrassment in the face of growing world criticism.

America was taking all the punches on the chin, without yet throwing one in return, and not surprisingly, the Russians were quick to seize their opportunity for anti-American propaganda. The Soviet government newspaper *Izvestia* launched its first verbal missiles by accusing the United States of 'reckless play with atomic bombs.' The attack was made in an article by Sergei Zykove, who wrote: 'The B-52 crash accentuates again the grave danger the flights of American bombers, with nuclear bombs aboard, represent to the security of the people. What happened in the area of Almeria, on January 17, may occur to-morrow at any place over West Europe, Asia, Africa or Latin America. While this catastrophe gave rise to indignation and alarm among the Spanish people, the Franco authorities tried to withhold the real nature of the accident from the population. The censorship did not let through even a short communiqué of the American military command.'

However, despite all provocation, the U.S. silence remained golden, and Admiral Guest concluded his conference just as General Bruce Halloway, Commander-in-Chief of the U.S. Air Force, in Europe, flew into Madrid from his headquarters at Wiesbaden, Germany. He was scheduled to have urgent talks with Ambassador Duke and General Donovan, chief of the American Military Mission, before they had a crucial meeting with the Spanish Air Minister, General Jose Lacalle Larraga.

A new crisis was looming. The future of all U.S. nuclear bomber flights over Spain was at stake.

*   *   *

At first light on Monday, January 24, Admiral Guest flew to 'Campamento Wilson', made several reconnaissance flights over the area, and some hours later clambered aboard a tiny rubber boat to ride out to the anchored minesweeper, U.S.S. Skill.

The initial units had already been assigned to Task Force

65 by Vice Admiral William E. Ellis, Commander of the Sixth Fleet. They included, apart from the four minesweepers already at the scene, the destroyer U.S.S Macdonough (DLG-8), which at first served as flagship and communications centre for Task Force 65, and the landing ship U.S.S. For Snelling (LSD-30), which was assigned to provide logistic support. The squat, 10,500-ton Fort Snelling, commanded by Captain I. A. Robinson, was later to prove to be of invaluable assistance, using her well-deck as a protective dock. The fleet tug U.S.S. Kiowa had returned to assist in lifting from the ocean floor debris which had been located by the frogmen, 'hard-hat' divers and minesweepers, and these ships were joined by the submarine rescue vessel U.S.S. Petrel (ASR-14), equipped with sonar for detecting underwater objects and with unique facilities for supporting diving search operations. The small oiler, U.S.S. Nespelen (AOG-55), also arrived to provide fuel for the Task Force.

Recovery of the two mysterious objects, reportedly at a depth of 2,000 feet, was far beyond the limits of the divers. Specialised equipment would obviously be required. Indeed, some of that equipment was already on its way to Palomares, along with experts from various parts of the world in the fields of ocean-ography, geology, salvage, ordnance, nuclear and biological science.

It was learned that the complex operation – on land and at sea – was costing a staggering one million dollars a day. It was, in fact, to become the biggest U.S. operation of the 1960's outside the Vietnamese war.

The state of uproar in the Pentagon persisted. Defence Department chiefs had been instructed to get hold of the best available equipment in the world, regardless of cost, and rush it to Spain. They set about tapping every possible source, so that, on the day Admiral Guest took command of the Task Force, the first item of specialised equipment from America had duly arrived by transport plane at the San Javier Air Academy base, near Cartagena. This delicate piece of equipment, looking rather like a bomb with outsize fins, was carefully transported to the beach-head, 90 miles away at Palomares. There it was taken aboard a landing craft, carried out to the minesweeper U.S.S. Pinnacle and immediately installed, to begin scanning the ocean floor.

This special equipment was, in fact, a towed sonar device

called Ocean Bottom Scanning Sonar (OBSS). It belonged to the Westinghouse Corporation, who were the first of eight civil contractors to respond to the appeal for help from the defence chiefs.

The OBSS was capable of operating at the fantastic, pressure-crushing depth of 20,000 feet, while scanning the terrain 260 feet on either side of its tow track and travelling at a speed of one knot, suspended by cable about 30 feet above the seabed. Its underwater 'magic-eye' was able to produce a pattern of highlights and shadows, using the ocean floor itself as a contrasting background for visual emphasis when locating objects.

It was joined by deepsea television, from the Naval Ordnance Test Station, Pasadena, California. The underwater television, with three telescope-shaped cameras, was suspended from a surface ship by cable and hovered two to three feet from the ocean floor, up to a maximum depth of 2,000 feet. A monitoring TV screen on deck enabled technicians to detect objects, evaluate them and generally to have a grandstand view of the bottom of the sea, with a 60 degree field of vision in all directions. Video tapes also assisted in later studies.

Another useful instrument was the Sea Scanner, an eight foot long metal post with two bulbous objects, rather like camping gas bottles, stuck on each end. This electronic echo-ranging and sounding device, owned by the Honeywell Corporation, was installed on 40 foot utility boats. It scanned ahead and to both sides of the boat at an angle between the surface of the sea and the bottom, projecting a high energy sound beam into the water. The beam could be pointed in any direction like an underwater searchlight or could be set to sweep automatically from side to side. Echoes reflected from underwater objects were thus detected, and the distance, direction and depth were shown on an indicator.

With the arrival of all this equipment the electronic search effort was intensified. The Spanish government gave rapid permission for the Americans to establish navigation reference stations ashore. The Navy Oceanographic division and the Commander of Service Squadron Eight despatched a group of technicians to assist in the installation of a precise electronic navigation system on existing charts. Errors, however, of up to 250 yards were soon discovered.

So the British Decca navigational system was utilised.

The concept of Decca was to provide accurate electronic positioning data in an area up to 200 miles from a master station. The system consisted of the master station, two slave stations, and indicating receivers on the ships that were to be positioned. Electronic signals from the master and slave stations were transmitted to a Decca receiver aboard ship, indicating the position of the vessel to within 10 feet.

The accuracy of geographical locating information in the salvage mission was of the utmost importance. If underwater contacts were to be investigated and retrieved from the seabed it was vital to pinpoint their location within inches. As the water depth increased, visibility and mobility decreased and navigational accuracy in the evaluation and recovery of material became essential. The Decca equipment greatly assisted the search units of Task Force 65.

As the weird gadgets began arriving by sea and air so, too, did the experts. They included men like Captain Horace C. Page, who was appointed Chief of Staff to Admiral Guest. The captain was well-qualified in the field of salvage and engineering, holding a master's degree in engineering from Rochester Polytechnic Institute, and he was one of the U.S. Navy's top specialists in salvage work. Prior to assuming his duties with Task Force 65 he was Fleet Maintenance and Salvage Officer for the Commander of the Sixth Fleet. He had served in various engineering assignments in the Navy since 1942 and had undertaken spells of duty at the naval shipyards in Charleston, South Carolina, and Norfolk, Virginia. He had been with the Navy's Bureau of Ships, prior to being posted to the Mediterranean area in 1964.

There was also the staff operations officer, Commander Roy M. Springer, who came from the Naval Analysis Group of the Office of Naval Research in Washington, D.C. He had served in five Navy submarines and had been commanding officer of the experimental submarine, U.S.S. Albacore (AGSS-569). The Navy had used Albacore to conduct research in underwater speed tests and on other experiments for the Bureau of Ships. In addition to his wide knowledge and experience in underwater operations and engineering, Commander Springer held a degree in electrical engineering from the Navy Post-Graduate School in Monterey, California.

Heading the team of more than 130 Navy divers assigned to the salvage operations was Lieutenant-Commander DeWitt 'Red' Moody. His extensive training included experience in deep-sea and Self Controlled Underwater Breathing Apparatus (SCUBA) diving. He was also a bomb disposal expert and had been sent to Palomares from Charleston, where he was commanding officer of Explosive Ordnance Disposal Unit Two. He brought to Task Force 65 a thorough knowledge of all types of weapons and was an authority on nuclear armament, having undergone special training in nuclear incident and accident procedures.

Flown in from San Diego, California, was a submariner and a former pilot of the bathyscaphe Trieste II, Lieutenant-Commander J. B. Mooney who was to become one of Admiral Guest's chief advisers. Mooney had served in three Navy submarines and had taught advanced tactics at the Navy's submarine school in New London, Connecticut. His most notable feat was in August, 1964, when he piloted the Trieste to a depth of 8,400 feet in the waters of the Atlantic, off Boston, Massachusetts, and found a major portion of the hull of the nuclear submarine, U.S.S. Thresher, which mysteriously vanished with the loss of 129 lives in April, 1963. More recently he had been in charge of Navy technicians assigned to Trieste and the Deep Submergence Group at San Diego.

In all, approximately twenty 'specialist' officers were assigned to the staff of the Task Force, and a total of about 2,200 men were attached to the various units and ships.

It was being proved that when disaster strikes, no nation is more effective in mounting a mammoth rescue operation than the United States. After taking all the punches, the Americans were starting to hit back.

*   *   *

In Palomares the ground trembled as snarling bulldozers, their caterpillar tracks churning up choking clouds of dust, strained to drag out chunks of embedded metal. Steel cables stretched almost to breaking point as the mechanical monsters slowly extracted whole jet engines, twisted and blackened beyond recognition, portions of silver wings, and lumps of fuselage.

Cranes and fork-lift trucks waited to hoist the wreckage on

to trucks, which then transported the finds to a bizarre dump alongside 'Campamento Wilson'. There it was all tipped on to the sand and airmen with geiger counters and alpha scintillation meters moved forward to make tests for signs of radioactivity.

Teams of crash investigators stood by to begin a meticulous examination of each piece of mangled metal, and every item, after being checked and examined, was labelled. Some objects were carefully put into plastic bags and sealed. Other, larger fragments were packed into big wooden crates.

Eventually, every single lump of metal recovered on land or from the sea, whether as small as a bottle top or as large as a car, was liable to be taken to the Torrejon airbase. There a U.S. Air Force disaster team, led by Colonel Carl Payne, made further examinations and worked on the plan that the B-52 should be reconstructed to determine how one of the engines caught fire and what caused the blaze to spread so quickly.

Outside Palomares cinema, villagers still queued up for radio-activity tests. Farmers now wishing to enter their fields in the restricted area were being allowed to do so. But they were ordered to wear radiation detector badges and before being allowed to return to their homes from the fields each night these were diligently checked.

Many of the millions of tomatoes were no longer a rosy red tinge. The sun had rotted them to an evil brown or black colour. Or was it the sun? Could they have been affected by radiation? The villagers did not know. All they did know was that they had been warned not to eat the local produce and religiously they refrained from doing so. They were too scared of the possible consequences if they did, and not even the sight of some of the American troops occasionally stopping to pick and eat tomatoes during their searches quelled the villagers' fears.

In any case, word had now spread like a plague among the inhabitants for miles around that vegetables from Palomares were 'contaminated'. Housewives were boycotting the markets with local produce for sale. Stocks of potatoes, onions, cabbages, cauliflowers and beans piled up. There were no takers when some stallholders even offered to give away their vegetables for nothing. Milk supplies turned sour, poultry sales dropped alarmingly and few dared to buy local eggs.

The fishermen were hit, too. They could not sell their catches.

With the possibility of a nuclear bomb nestling on the seabed where the fisherman normally cast their nets, villagers firmly believed the sardines and shrimps would be poisoned.

At Mojacar, the Norlands were on the verge of quitting their new home because of the radioactivity fears. 'We were scared stiff when we realised that a nuclear bomb had virtually landed on our doorstep,' said Mrs Norland. 'And it was really frightening when we were told that some villagers in Palomares – about ten families, I believe – had been evacuated from their homes because of danger of radiation. We seriously considered leaving Mojacar and returning to England.'

Her husband went down to the crash zone to investigate. 'Like ourselves, all the villagers were frightened to death in Mojacar,' he said. 'We were scared to eat the vegetables in case they had been contaminated. The Americans, however, seemed quite casual about the whole thing. They told me there was nothing to worry about so I returned to the village and assured everyone not to panic.'

Emergency food supplies were being shipped into the area. At the local stores, supplies of tin openers ran out as more and more people 'played it safe' by purchasing tinned foods.

Furthermore, it was suggested in New York by a top U.S. nuclear scientist that the B-52 crash could pose an 'indirect' danger to the health of inhabitants in the region.

Doctor Hans Bethe, one of the original architects of the Hiroshima atom bomb, told John Gold, American-based correspondent of the London *Evening News*, that the threat would arise if the missing bomb broke up, scattering radio active plutonium.

The 59-year-old scientist, speaking at the Cornell University in Ithaca, New York, emphasised that cancer-producing plutonium would not be dangerous merely on contact. To be dangerous, it would have to be consumed and absorbed by the human body, via contaminated food.

'Less than one milligramme, if it were eaten, could get into the bones and cause bone cancer,' he warned. 'One milligramme is awfully little. You could barely see it. On the other hand, if proper precautions were taken, it would be extremely unlikely for anyone to eat it.'

Doctor Bethe, wartime director of the theoretical physics

division at Los Alamos and a member of the President's Science Advisory Committee, qualified assurances by Washington's defence chiefs that nuclear weapons, because they were unarmed, would prove harmless in a bomber crash.

'The Defence Department always says that such a bomb cannot go off accidentally,' he said. 'This is perfectly correct. The impact of a crash will not trigger it. But if the bomb breaks up – and that is likely in a crash such as the one in Spain – the plutonium might scatter to some extent, with the possiblity of harmful effects.'

What were the dangers if a nuclear bomb had landed in the Mediterranean? 'Certainly no radiation would get up through the sea to any person,' Doctor Bethe went on. 'But if the device is destroyed, which again is possible, some of the plutonium might float in the sea. This, however, would be in such small concentrations that I would think it would be entirely harmless.

'There is a remote possibility that some fish might absorb some of the plutonium. But it is unlikely they would take in enough to cause any danger to humans. The plutonium would be in the bones of the fish anyway, and people would be unlikely to eat the bones.'

Many of the villagers of Palomares, however, had drawn their own conclusions and were sticking to them. They had nagging doubts about possible food danger, and nothing would alter their minds.

The farmers became angry as their hard-worked crops rotted away in front of their eyes, and it was to smooth their rising tempers and to dispel their alarm at the prospect of incurring big financial losses, that the U.S. government speedily set about the task of paying out huge sums in compensation.

An Air Force lawyer was appointed by the U.S. 16th Air Force to investigate all hardship claims. His name was Lieutenant-Colonel Joseph G. Stulb and he set up his office in a small tent near the beach.

Immediately he purchased nearly 4,500 pounds of unwanted tomatoes for £110 cash, a popular transaction which helped to ease much of the tension which had been building up between the local inhabitants and intruding American forces. He also took over the handling of daily payments to unemployed farmhands and the out-of-pocket fishermen of Villaricos.

All his payments – up to a maximum of £5,200 for individual claims – were made in cash. Villagers lined up outside the claims tent-office, clutching grubby pieces of paper on which they had scrawled the income they would have expected to receive from their crops. They arrived on foot, by donkey, in horse-drawn carts, and, the more prosperous, by Land Rover or tractor.

When summoned inside the darkened tent they sat down on a rickety wooden chair facing the colonel across a small camp table and with expressive waves of the hand, shrugs of the shoulders and a torrent of rapid-fire Andalusian Spanish, presented their cases.

Colonel Stulb would listen sympathetically, jotting down notes. Then, when he had heard sufficient explanations and measured the degree of exaggeration, if any, of the claim, he made his decision. With a flourish he would reach over to a leather case at his side, flick open the catch, produce a wad of green 1,000 peseta notes, worth almost £6 each, and make an on-the-spot settlement.

These emergency payment measures served to bridge a gap while the governments of American and Spain thrashed out the details of more substantial compensation, involving all factors resulting from the crash.

But across the coffee-stained wooden table in Colonel Stulb's little tent it is estimated that some £300,000 was eventually handed over in compensation claims.

As one of the American airmen on guard duties near the claims tent so aptly put it: 'The farmers will have nothing to worry about now. They should be thinking about what kind of car they'll be able to buy next month.'

*   *   *

The food scare was not only confined to the province of Almeria. Now that details were being published, partially disclosing what had happened in Palomares, housewives throughout Spain were becoming increasingly fussy and selective during their shopping expeditions.

'Where are these tomatoes from? Not from Palomares? Are they safe to eat?' were some of the questions most frequently posed to stallholders in the markets.

Amid all the suspicions and speculations it was decided on Monday, January 24 – exactly a week after the crash – to issue another soothing statement from Torrejon. It said: 'Elements of the U.S. Navy and U.S. Army are assisting Spanish authorities and the U.S. Air Force in the search for wreckage of the B-52 and KC-135, which suffered an accident during a refuelling mission.

'Air Force officials reconfirm that radiological surveys have found no indication of danger to public health or safety as a result of the accident.'

But trouble was coming to the boil. The fears of ambassador Duke, of anti-American feelings running high and of possible demonstrations, were not ill-founded. Left-wing students at the University of Madrid were planning a giant protest march to the American embassy in an attempt to force the closure of the military bases in Spain. Thousands of pamphlets were being distributed at University City, and the Monarchist daily newspaper *ABC* reported that some of these had been signed by the Central Committee of the outlawed Spanish Communist Party. The Young Christian Democrats – a clandestine students organisation – also issued a declaration protesting at 'the situation of United States' atomic colonialism over the peninsular.'

It was to this background of simmering unrest that General Halloway, the European-based U.S. Air Force chief – on his first visit to Spain since assuming command – kept his appointment with the Spanish Air Minister.

Although the U.S. 16th Air Force claimed that the general's presence in Madrid was not connected with the nuclear bomber crash, it became obvious within the next 24 hours that his trip from Wiesbaden was not merely 'routine'.

For it was then learned that as a direct result of the crash all nuclear bomber flights of the Strategic Air Command over Spain had been suspended indefinitely. Apparently, the flights had been stopped on the same day as the B-52 disaster. Now, technical studies were being made to determine if S.A.C. flights could be re-routed as much as possible over the sea instead of over the land.

Neither Torrejon nor the American ambassador would confirm the reported suspension. Said Mr William Bell, the Information Officer at the U.S. embassy: 'It is not in the national interest to discuss the movement of nuclear armament.'

But four days later, after a 12-hour cabinet session at the Cortes when the Air Minister, General Lacalle Larraga, presented a confidential report to General Franco, the confirmation at last came out.

All flights by the bombers over Spain had been prohibited at the request of the Spanish government.

'The prohibition is permanent,' explained Senor Manuel Fraga Iribarne, the Spanish Information Minister. 'The ban could, however, be lifted during an emergency by the mutual consent of the two governments.'

Senor Iribarne emphasised that the decision to halt the flights had been carried out after 'cordial' discussions between American and Spanish government officials.

It remained to be seen if other European countries, which allowed U.S. nuclear bomber over-flights, would follow the Spanish example.

The decision, as far as Spain was concerned, was certainly a bold one. Franco relied heavily on American military and economic aid, yet here he was risking his country's security by spiking the guns, or rather nuclear bombs, of the 24-hour U.S. global patrols poised against the threat of an attack from the East.

The ban could have meant the eventual shut-down of the three S.A.C. bases at Torrejon, Zaragoza and Moron, near Seville and, perhaps, a drastic cut in aid to Spain. Only one bargaining card and link with America would remain: the £33 million Rota Naval Base, near Cadiz, on the Atlantic coast, where U.S. submarines armed with nuclear-tipped Polaris missiles were stationed.

Although the complex of S.A.C. bases might be of no more use as stopover places and the bombers would have to refuel over international waters by-passing Spain, the depot for submarines at Rota, not affected by the ban, assuredly retained its importance.

Franco, as shrewd as ever after almost 27 years of dictatorial rule, was well aware of the dilly-dallyings of President Charles de Gaulle, of France, with his dreams of an independent nuclear striking force. If de Gaulle did go ahead with his plans and quit N.A.T.O. then the Americans would be forced to look elsewhere to station their vast squadrons of jet interceptor fighters.

So Spain's decision to request the nuclear flight ban without arousing the wrath of the U.S. government was a calculated risk. Franco realised that soon the Americans could be fully expected to cut down on the thousands of servicemen stationed in Spain, as a prelude to the closing down of the S.A.C. bases which were now almost outdated by the advance of nuclear warfare.

But he held two trump cards. One, the U.S. would certainly not seek to cancel its pact with Spain when it again expired in September, 1968, because Rota, from a tactical defence point of view, was too vital to abandon. And, two, Franco was confident that the first place the Americans would seek to station their jet fighters, if thrown out of France, would be in Spain.

Then, the military and economic ties between the two countries would be immeasurably stronger than ever. It was clever diplomacy.

*   *   *

Still the ships kept steaming in to join Task Force 65. Latest addition was the arrival, on January 26, of the oceanographic survey vessel U.S.N.S. Dutton (TAGS-11), whose skipper was immediately assigned the responsibility by Admiral Guest of charting the ocean bottom throughout the search area.

The Navy's Oceanographic Department Two, aboard the Dutton, assisted in ensuing 36-day operation by providing the best possible charts for navigators and plotting contacts suspected of being debris.

During the establishment of the navigation stations and the hydrographic survey of the ocean, three of the four minesweepers initially swept the area down to 900 feet. From the fourth, the U.S.S. Pinnacle, the Ocean Bottom Scanning Sonar device was used to probe beyond these depths.

Among the Underwater Demolition Teams (UDT) working from the beach, two bearded frogmen suddenly appeared. Even the American airmen at 'Campamento Wilson' were convinced the British Navy had been called in to lend a hand. But, as it turned out, they were two U.S. Navy SCUBA divers, David Lane and James Bloecel, both from Charleston, South Carolina.

The divers combed the inshore areas. Later, after an initial search of the 'high probability' areas, search patterns were extended and some areas were searched visually by divers and others electronically by the minesweepers with their sonar and by OBSS devices.

Frogmen and SCUBA divers adopted various methods of searching the inshore waters to a depth of 200 feet. Kicking out with their black rubber fins they moved shoulder to shoulder through the water, peering down to the seabed through their oval-shaped face masks. Some of the divers held lines, knotted at regular intervals, the spacing of which was regulated by the visibility of the underwater area to be searched. This not only allowed the men to keep a constant distance between themselves but made it easier to record the area covered.

In some areas the divers followed lines towed by surface vessels and charted their search zones by the position of the boats in reference to electronic navigational aids. At one time, over 130 divers were taking part in the giant undersea hunt – silent black shadows flitting through the sparkling blue water like prowling sharks. 'Hard-hat' divers, sweating inside their weighted, cumbersome suits, investigated inky depths up to 264 feet.

Chunks of recovered wreckage ranged in size from pieces as small as a postage stamp to whole wing sections. Each precious item was hauled, dripping, out of the sea, placed carefully aboard a landing craft and then taken to the dump ashore for radioactivity checks and eventual transportation to Torrejon.

Aboard his destroyer flagship U.S.S. Macdonough, Admiral Guest sifted through every scrap of incoming information, including detailed reports by the pilot and three crew survivors of the B-52 and eyewitness accounts given by a handful of civilians. Among these was the description by fisherman Francisco Simo of what he had seen fall from the sky on the morning of the crash. The Admiral, as he flicked over the pages of the reports, was immediately interested by the fisherman's observations.

Captain Page, his Chief-of-Staff, was asked to arrange for an officer and two men to go to the port of Aguilas and accompany Senor Simo in his trawler to the exact spot where he had noticed the parachutes, with their strange-looking cargoes, splash down and sink.

As the surveys and searches continued, the difficulties of exploring the rugged, mountainous undersea terrain in the 120 square mile salvage area became more apparent. There were canyons, with murky depths, of well over 3,600 feet. The bottom was composed of silt in some areas and thick mud in others. Generally, below the ooze was hard metallic rock – virtually an underwater minefield – which tended to make nonsense of the delicate electronic readings of the sonar devices.

Admiral Guest, if he was to carry out his three-phase task successfully – to search and locate wreckage, to verify and mark it with red and orange-coloured buoys, and then to make the actual recovery – was in dire need of more underwater devices with grappling attachments, whether tested or experimental, from U.S. Navy or commercial enterprises.

Several contacts had already been made at depths beyond 500 feet. The problem remained: How to raise these objects – perhaps, among them, the missing bomb – from the seabed?

In Washington, the Defence Department was preparing to ship a bathyscaphe to Palomares. Already on its way to Spain was an underwater Deep Jeep – similar to the craft described in Ian Flemings' book 'Thunderball' – which was a white vessel shaped like a fat cigar and about as long as a mini-car. The Deep Jeep, suspended by cable from a ship, was able to cruise under its own power beneath the waves. It was equipped with lights and television cameras.

But these Jules Verne-like creations, although able to spot objects hundreds of fathoms down on the ocean bed, were not able to recover anything because they were without grappling equipment. So late on Thursday, January 27, Mr Robert McNamara, the U.S. Secretary of Defence, still pondering on a solution to the embarrassing situation in Spain, gave instructions for two key phone calls to be made. The first was to the Office of Naval Research and the second to the Reynolds Aluminium Corporation, in Florida.

Less than 24 hours later, Defence chiefs announced that the world's two most advanced search submarines would soon be on their way to join the big Palomares hunt.

The midget vessels, described as 'submersibles', were the silver Alvin, built by the Applied Sciences Division of Litton Industries exclusively for naval research, and the bright orange and dark blue Aluminaut, which cost £1 million to construct.

The Alvin, 22 feet long and weighing a mere 13 tons, was able to dive down to 6,000 feet and stay below for a maximum of 24 hours. She was equipped with magnetic compass, fathometer, ground detector, sonar telephone system, scanning sonar and closed circuit television. A telescopic grappling claw could also be attached. Inside the seven-foot diameter pressure sphere of high-strength steel, 1.33″ thick, there was sufficient room for a pilot and two observers to crouch among an impressive battery of switches, knobs, dials, television screens and instrument panels. The Alvin, with a submerged range of 15 to 20 miles, had a top speed of four knots.

The Aluminaut, the world's deepest diving submarine, capable of operating nearly three miles down for 32 hours at a time, was much larger, being 51 feet long and weighing 81 tons. She was equipped with underwater telephones, an electronic fathometer, continuous transmission frequency-modulated scanning sonar, bottom scanning sonar, underwater illumination equipment, a trainable television camera, gyro compass, and grotesque, nine-foot-long robot arms to grab objects on the seabed. She could carry an operating crew of two men and four passengers, plus a scientific instrumentation payload of 6,000 pounds. Maximum speed was 3.8 knots.

Two cargo planes were being prepared to fly the Alvin to Spain from the Otis Air Force Base in Falmouth, Massachusetts. It was a C-133 which was to carry the vessel's bulbous fuselage while the conning tower, with its large observation window in front, was to be transported in a C-141. Mr William Rainnie, 41-year-old chief pilot and project co-ordinator at the Woods Hole Oceanographic Institute, was standing by to head a 12-man team of scientists accompanying the Alvin on its mission.

The Aluminaut, owned by Reynolds Submarine Services Corporation and launched in 1965, was still undergoing tests at Miami. Her crew had been alerted to sail for Spain as soon as a Navy landing ship dock could be prepared for the 3,000-mile Atlantic crossing. Her skipper, usually, was 42-year-old, 6 feet 2 inches tall Frederick Dutton, a former U.S. Navy submariner, father of six children, and a determined character who invariably wore a ten gallon hat and a Texas string tie on his expeditions under the sea.

The Navy, it was learned, had contracted to pay a staggering

£28,000 fee for each 30 days hire of this aluminium vessel, originally manufactured by the Electric Boat Division of General Dynamics Corporation, and which had recently set a diving record of 6,500 feet, although it was designed to work at depths up to 15,000 feet.

The Defence chiefs were secretly delighted to have acquired the services of the two midget 'super subs', yet they still remained stubbornly silent when asked if the vessels would be used to try and recover a lost nuclear warhead. They refused to reveal the number of weapons which had been carried aboard the crashed B-52 or confirm the reports that three bombs had been recovered, while one was still missing. Consequently, they also declined to reveal whether the 'nuclear armament' had been four hydrogen bombs of 25 megaton capacity.

In any case, time was now becoming an all-important factor in the hunt, and there were nagging doubts about the success of the operation, even when the Alvin and Aluminaut arrived at the search area. Oceanographers repeatedly warned that with every passing day, tides and currents would make salvage more difficult, burying objects in the Mediterranean silt and mud.

Then, there was the added problem of what would happen if the two submersibles actually spotted the bomb. The Alvin was still apparently awaiting delivery of its attachable grappling claw. And the Aluminaut's famed articulated arms were back at a General Electric plant for modifications. The mechanical claws could be flown to the spot in time for the hunt. But they still might not be of any use.

'With luck the Aluminaut's crew could use its robot arms to attach a line to a chunk of plane wreckage,' confided Mr Lloyd Morris, Operations Manager of Reynolds Submarine Services, 'but it is possible they might not be strong enough to lift anything as heavy as an H-bomb.'

There was a more sinister reason for having the subs on the spot as soon as possible, as Doctor Bethe, the U.S. nuclear scientist, pointed out. Asked why such an intensive hunt was apparently being made for an apparently harmless bomb which, according to the experts, could not explode, he warned:

'*There is the danger that someone else might find it intact and learn how it is made.*

'It is not a time bomb. That is, you can go there and work

on it and there is no danger that it will explode in your face. I would imagine that if somebody found the thing intact and really tried hard, then he could set it off. I see no reason why this could not be so.'

If this was the case, a foreign power could nip in and scoop the sunken bomb – possibly an ultra high security weapon – from the grasp of the Americans. And then discover its secrets! Doctor Bethe's theory was not so far out.

The Soviet naval threat in the Mediterranean had grown to alarming proportions during recent years. Russian cruisers, destroyers, submarines and even Kynda-class guided missile frigates had been detected sneaking furtively along the sea routes.

Democratic Senator Stuart Symington issued a stern warning about this later, when a heavily censored report which he had made to the Senate Armed Services and Foreign Relations Committee, was made public. He said: 'The Russians have made a respectable start in becoming a first-rate naval power. They are learning their operating lessons well, and they must be taken seriously. The Soviet threat in the Mediterranean does not stop with the actual Soviet units. Through a large naval aid programme, Soviet naval units are found in the navies of several Mediterranean countries, including Algeria, Egypt, Syria, Cyprus and Yugoslavia.'

Admiral Guest was well aware of the Russian menace. That was one of the reasons why a Soviet trawler, which had been lurking for several months in the international waters near the top-secret Polaris submarine base at Rota, on the Atlantic coast, was now being kept under 24-hour surveillance.

That innocent-looking trawler was, in fact, bristling with radar, carried highly sensitive electronic sonar for scanning the seabed, and one morning shortly before dawn slipped anchor, and, with a turn of speed remarkable for an apparently sluggish fishing vessel, steamed smartly off in the direction of the Straits of Gibraltar – towards Palomares.

The prospect of netting an errant nuclear bomb appeared to be tempting bait for the Red spy ship. A big catch indeed, for the Kremlin!

CHAPTER FIVE

I WILL NEVER forget the stranger-than-fiction activities I witnessed on my first trip to Palomares.

Almost two weeks had elapsed since the nuclear bomber crash and in that time Fleet Street, the nerve centre of Britain's newspapers in London, E.C.4, had taken a surprisingly off-hand interest in the story.

Initially, the fact that possibly four H-bombs had cascaded down on Spain's south west holiday coast had been greeted with detached coolness. The implications just did not register.

The foreign editor of one mass circulation daily newspaper, for example, rebuked his Madrid correspondent who excitedly phoned through with a vivid, 300-word report. 'Keep it down to a paragraph, old boy,' he instructed, soothingly. 'After all, the bombs didn't explode did they?'

An incredible decision! Here was perhaps one of the major stories of the year being reduced to a sentence. Ironically, a few days later, that same editor was to find himself gripped with excitement and hastily despatching one of his star writers from London to Palomares to try and catch up with the news he had previously rejected.

I was luckier than some of the foreign correspondents based in Spain, who encountered the early disinterest. The London *Daily Express* kept an alert eye on all developments and as soon as it was revealed that the subs Alvin and Aluminaut were being rushed to Spain, I was instructed to depart immediately to the scene.

Palomares was perhaps the most inaccessible place in Spain. The nearest civil airport was at Malaga, a tortuous, six-hour coastal drive away. There was no direct train service except by express to either Murcia or Granada, both approximately ten-hour journeys. Upon arrival at these two cities there was the wearying prospect of taxi trips of at least 100 miles to the village.

There was no other speedy solution than to drive the 365 long miles from Madrid to Palomares. I set off with my wife Georgina – the feminine eye for detail and ear for information were to prove a valuable asset on this assignment – at 11 a.m. on the busy N IV highway, the main road artery connecting the Spanish capital with the coastal resorts of the south. The road, despite the rumbling transport lorries plying back and forth with their deliveries of fresh fish, fruit and vegetables and the sun-seeking tourists in their cars from all over Europe, is fast although pitted with those bone-jarring potholes invariably found on most Spanish highways.

Whereas the pale sun had shone meekly in Madrid, it now blazed strongly. In Murcia, the next big city beyond Albacete, the sweet aroma of orange blossom filled the air like a heavy cloud of perfume. The cobbled road on the final lap to the coast swept past rich and fertile horticultural land where many lemons, oranges, peaches and apricots ripened. Palm trees gently swayed a rhythm in the warm breeze, crickets chattered merrily in the olive groves, and barbary figs, a dark shiny green, hung from the branches of gnarled trees.

In front of our car, a big, blue U.S. Air Force bus, followed by two heavily-laden, tarpaulin-covered trucks, suddenly emerged on to the main road from the direction of the San Javier Air Academy. Another fifty airmen and more equipment was on its way to the beach-head.

The villages of Totana, Lorca and Puerto Lumbreras, cradled in the foothills of the Sierra Espuna range, swept by in rapid succession. The road noticeably deteriorated, with dried-up riverbeds cutting right across the tarmac at regular intervals, and subsidences obviously caused by torrents of water having gushed down from the hills during infrequent but torrential storms. The ground, hard-packed, dry and unable to absorb the rainwater had consequently become rutted. For 30 miles, the car pitched and tossed on the humps, tyres squealing, brakes protesting, rather like a rough ride on the big dipper at a fairground.

It was past 5.30 p.m. when we finally neared Palomares, but it was my intention to visit the American camp before nightfall. Already the light was fast failing with the sun, a hazy red, sinking below the horizon. Impulsively, I turned off the road on to a bumpy cart-track which wound through orange groves and tomato fields in the direction of the sea.

The car's wheels churned up clouds of choking dust which seemed to penetrate everywhere despite the windows being closed and the ventilation shut off. Vision in the rear view mirror was completely obliterated as the dust spiralled high in the air. The earth, apart from the areas of irrigated farmland, had been bleached almost white by the sun and it had obviously not tasted a single drop of rain for several months, or perhaps years.

For almost three miles, we drove along that narrow, twisting track past isolated farm buildings and cave dwellings which had been carved in the barren hillsides and where poverty-stricken peasants still eked out an existence. There was not a soul in sight. Then, as we rounded a bend at the top of a shingle slope, we could just make out, about a mile in the distance, clusters of tiny white-washed houses. The seven-hour journey was almost over. This was Palomares.

I drove cautiously. Everywhere was strangely silent. There was no sign of any villagers, and the fields, many of them marked with the tiny red flags, were deserted. Even in the half light we could see hundreds of tomatoes rotting away on their stalks.

We also noticed that the track was now no longer dusty. From a point about half-a-mile from the edge of the village it was damp as if it had been specially sprayed with water. There were fresh wheel tracks. We had obviously approached Palomares via the backdoor. The track seemed to divert across the rocky and bone dry Almanzora riverbed in the direction of Villaricos, the small fishing village alongside Palomares. The ground was still damp, the wheel tracks still very clear. At regular intervals, guards were standing on duty, but we continued unchallenged.

Suddenly, a big red truck came bumping down the track towards us. I steered the car aside to let it pass. It was a water wagon and an airman, clinging tightly to the rails of a platform at the back, was adjusting the nozzles of the sprays pumping gallons of water on to the ground. There was something odd about that airman. He was wearing conventional khaki fatigues and a black beret but his trousers had been tucked inside his muddied boots and tape had been used to seal any gaps between cloth and leather. All the pockets on his fatigues had been taped up, too. Odder still, his sideburns had also been covered up by the white, shiny plastic tape.

At this precise moment a haulage lorry lurched into view over the rise about 100 yards behind the water wagon. It was transporting a large, sealed, wooden crate. It seemed highly unlikely that it was carrying tomatoes or other local produce in such a strange container, particularly as the driver was wearing a white protective overall and a face mask.

This lorry was followed by another and another – six in all, each loaded with a wooden crate. The drivers in their cabs each wore masks and white overalls. The weird convoy roared noisily past our parked car, and we could then see that flaps at the rear of the crates had been bolted shut. What was in the containers? We could not find out then.

We drove on. At the top of the rise we were less than a mile from the sea. In the sweeping half-moon-shaped bay of the Gulf of Vera could be seen the twinkling lights of four big warships with their revolving scanners, protruding aerials and masts. A little further along the cart track was an old fort, with what appeared to be tents pitched alongside. Slowly we approached the Moorish fort. There seemed to be about 20 men digging near the tents not far from a tilted flagstaff from which a bright orange pennant drooped. What did this mean?

Less than 100 yards from the fort, the scene became somewhat macabre. It was rather like observing gravediggers silently at work in a cemetery. Each of the men was energetically digging. They all wore white protective clothing, as had the lorry drivers, as well as rubber taped boots and blue face masks. Airmen in fatigues stood by with what looked like geiger counters and other electronic equipment, occasionally stooping down to point the gadgets at the heaps of shovelled earth. As the men dug, water was being hosed on to the dry soil.

We did not have any more time to find out what was going on. Two Spanish guards came running towards the car.

'Que necesita usted?' demanded one of the guards. 'What do you want? Where are your documents?'

I fumbled to produce my British Press card from my wallet. 'Periodista, huh!' he snorted, contemptuously. 'You cannot stay here. Go away, immediately!'

An American military policeman and two Spaniards in civilian clothes came running towards us.

'I am afraid this is a restricted area,' said the police sergeant in a breathless drawl. 'I must ask you to leave at once. I cannot allow you to observe the work going on here.

'These two men,' he added, indicating his two scowling companions, 'are Spanish security police. I should do as I say or you might find yourselves in serious trouble.'

As I reversed the car to return along the track, I noticed that some of the earth being dug out of a large pit was being placed in metal containers and taken into a tent which had orange-coloured, plastic windows. More men were working under the canvas.

One of the Spanish guards was instructed by his senior officer to get into our car and escort us out of the forbidden zone. He directed us back towards Palomares.

It transpired that the men in masks were scientists and had been digging for radio active objects – possibly parts of one of the bombs – and these were being placed together with contaminated dirt into the crates, after on-the-spot tests, for transportation to a secret destination. They wore the 'moon' suits, masks and taped boots to keep the deadly dust particles, perhaps infected with alpha rays, away from their skin.

*   *   *

Incredibly, the midget sub Alvin was snowbound! After a week-end of hasty preparation, the Alvin, dismantled in two sections, was finally all set to be flown from the United States to the Polaris submarine base at Rota, near Gibraltar, from where it would be taken by ship to join the bomb hunt.

The chief pilot, Mr Rainnie, had closely supervised the loading of the fuselage aboard the Cargomaster transport plane, while the conning tower had been gently manoeuvred into the bay of the C-141.

Ten scientists, including the two pilots of the submersible, 41-year-old Mr Valentine P. Wilson and Mr Marvin J. McCamis, 43, both from Falmouth, Massachusetts, were ready for departure.

Only hours before take-off, however, on Monday morning January 31, freak snowstorms swept across America and enveloped the Otis Air Force Base at Falmouth. The planes were grounded. So bleak was the weather forecast that it seemed likely that several days might elapse before the Alvin could be flown to Spain. It was a blow to the anxious Defence chiefs. The other submarine, the Aluminaut, had not yet been loaded aboard a U.S. Navy landing ship dock in Florida.

Faced with this new crisis the Defence Department decided to despatch yet another tiny underwater craft to Palomares, the Perry Cubmarine PC-3B submersible, owned by Ocean Systems, Incorporated.

The yellow-painted Cubmarine was a two-man vessel, capable of diving to maximum depths of 600 feet, for periods of up to six hours and travelling at a speed of two knots. Equipped with underwater telephone, gyro compass and fathometer its main task would be to release marker buoys when objects were located on the sea bed.

It would be several days before the Cubmarine could be sent across the Atlantic. Even this craft had its limitations, and it would hardly be able to lift an H-bomb from the seabed.

The crux of the matter was that the U.S. Navy's budget had been drastically slashed earlier in the year for economy reasons and no proper equipment was available or had been tested to undertake such a task efficiently. When the nuclear submarine Thresher went down off Boston there was the same sort of problem. The Navy had rapidly to assemble a make-shift search fleet, and it took months to find the crushed hull which could not be raised because of the tremendous depth.

The tragedy of the Thresher resulted in the Navy being given the go-ahead for a 250-million-dollar programme to build craft capable of finding and rescuing the crews of submarines trapped in crushing depths as great as 3,500 feet. The programme set two targets with a 1969 completion date; to develop a system of finding and recovering objects as large as a plane or nuclear missiles and bombs from depths of 20,000 feet, and to enable men to tackle salvage work at depths ranging between 600–800 feet outside their submarines.

The Navy made some successful progress with the Sealab experiments enabling divers to operate on the seabed as deep as 800 feet. In 1964 Sealab I was lowered in 194 feet of water off Bermuda with four divers staying down for 11 days. Then, in 1965, Sealab II went down 205 feet off La Jolla, California, with three 10-man teams taking turns at 15-day shifts below the waves.

These experiments gave scientists the vital answers of how to keep men on the ocean floor for a month or longer, breathing a mixture of gas that was largely helium. With special equipment, the men were also able to work outside their undersea craft for an hour or more.

Further Sealab projects were planned. Eventually it was hoped to commandeer a nuclear submarine, probably one that was built to launch the now obsolete Regulus missile, so that the 80-foot by 34-foot pressure chamber that housed the missile could easily be adapted for the use of divers.

The Navy's top priority deep submergence programme also allowed for the building of six small submarines, each about 40 feet long, weighing 25 tons and able to cruise underwater for up to 12 hours. They would be clamped to a normal-sized nuclear submarine – rather like the tiny fish that cluster around a whale or dolphin – and at a disaster scene could be released. The midget vessels would be able to attach themselves, limpet style, on to the escape hatch of the stricken craft and rescue 12 men at a time by ferrying them back to the sister submarine.

One of the toughest problems still to be solved was that of perfecting the high resolution sonar for giving rescuers a close-up picture of bombs or crippled submarines. Underwater television was fine in crystal clear waters, but with sediment clouding on the seabed its range of vision could be cut to a mere 4 inches.

So, all in all, the Navy's chore of tracking down and hauling up the H-bomb, probably lying somewhere offshore from Palomares, was a formidable task. None of the Sealab equipment, for example, was available on an operational scale. The Defence chiefs were fully aware that the entire operation might be doomed to dismal failure. But, with the threat constantly posed by the presence of the Russian trawler and the sheer embarrassment of the whole affair, they had to gamble on success with the three tiny submersibles to find the bomb.

In any case, there was, apparently, another disturbing reason behind the flap at the Pentagon.

This was revealed in an exclusive front page 'splash' story in the *Daily Mirror*, which was never denied. A report from

Washington claimed that the missing bomb was not the only target of the search and that some black boxes, vital to Western security and which should have been destroyed automatically in the crash, were lost.

'The B-52 carried black boxes to put out phoney signals to upset radar defences and ward off attacking rockets,' the report declared. 'There were more boxes to work out secret flight routes and target details if an attack was ordered.

'The boxes would decide whether a bomb would be exploded either in the air or on the ground. And there were black boxes dealing with the codes by which bomber captains get their orders.

'The possibility that this equipment might still be intact where it could be found by an unfriendly power is deeply embarrassing.'

*   *   *

I was soon to discover that Palomares and the villages for several miles around were infested and crawling with extraordinary numbers of agents attached to the Direccion General de Seguridad, Franco's equivalent to the Special Branch at Scotland yard, M.I.5, or C.I.A.

Spain certainly seemed to be taking seriously the possibility of Soviet spies prowling in the vicinity, stumbling over the lost bomb and perhaps even stealing the warhead, or finding the black boxes.

At 'Campamento Wilson' journalists questioned Colonel Young. The colonel, in blue, zip-pocketed fatigues, drew circles in the sand with a broken twig as he wearily chanted out the replies.

Question: 'How many ships are there offshore today, colonel?'

Answer: 'Ships? All I can say is that certain elements of the U.S. Navy are here.'

Q: 'Has the missing bomb been found yet?'

A: 'I know absolutely nothing about a lost bomb.'

Q: 'When will the recovery submarines arrive, colonel?'

A: 'No comment.' Then, after a pause. 'Do you really think you're going to see them. They won't make low passes over Palomares you know. They don't fly.'

Q: 'Is there any risk of radiation, or are you merely taking precautions?'

A: 'No comment.'

Q: 'Where can we get information, colonel?'

A: 'From me,' Another pause. Then: 'I have no comment to make about anything and I cannot comment on why I have to say no comment.'

Q: 'All right, colonel, if you cannot comment, can you answer this one question? How would you, as a journalist, rate the story of this incident at Palomares?'

The colonel, staring at the circles in the sand, thought hard for a moment. Then, pointing the twig to emphasise his words, he replied: 'Well, I think that this is the greatest story ever . . . if it is ever told.'

From this point on the conversation degenerated back to the ceaseless string of 'No comments.'

Colonel 'No Information' Young did nothing to endear himself to the world's Press representatives who later descended in scores upon the camp. Admittedly, he was acting under orders, but, with the Defence Department remaining tight-lipped, his much-quoted and negative words caused considerable damage to the American image in the face of world suspicions and fears about the H-bomb incident.

Columnist Cassandra – alias Sir William Connor, of the London *Daily Mirror* – exercised his dry, rapier wit to take 'Lieutenant Colonel Chatterbox, this blabberer, this loquacious spokesman' to task.

'So you want to know whether the Americans have really recovered the hydrogen bomb that has been missing since one of their aircraft crashed?' he wrote. 'The first answer is that they positively have recovered the bomb. The second answer is that they positively haven't recovered the bomb.

'I have this from the highest possible source, a man implicitly trusted by the top security officers in Washington.

'. . . Colonel Young is the voice of America minus the vocal chords. He is the big say-so who never says-so. He has a line in negative conversation that is in a class of its own.

'. . . That is why the bomb that has been recovered has not been recovered. That is why it emits radiation and does not emit radiation. That is why a valuable piece of the firing mechanism of the bomb has been recovered and has also not been recovered.

'And, if you ask me why I have no comment to make about anything, I cannot comment on why I have no comment to comment on, why I have no comment to comment about anything.

'Everything quite clear now?'

* * *

The tall, slim man with the boyishly handsome face had only just arrived at the bustling Kennedy Airport after flying in from Lagos, Nigeria, aboard a silver, four-engined Boeing jet.

It was bitterly cold and he tugged the warm collar of his blue overcoat protectively under his chin. As he walked briskly from the customs building he was intercepted by a man who handed him a letter.

He was tired after the long flight and was looking forward to greeting his wife and spending a quiet week-end with his three sons and two daughters at their home in Seattle, Washington.

The contents of that letter, however, were destined to change drastically his carefully-laid plans. He read it through, folded the crisp sheet of notepaper back in the envelope, and then headed towards a phone booth.

Jon Lindbergh, 33-year-old son of the world-famous air pioneer who made the first non-stop flight from New York to Paris in the monoplane 'Spirit of St Louis', would not be going home after all.

Whereas his father, Charles A. Lindbergh, had triumphed in the air, his son had made a name for himself under the sea.

That letter, handed over in New York, was from his company, Ocean Systems, Incorporated, with whom he was a branch manager of their Pacific Northwest Division.

Along with the pilots of the submersible, Cubmarine – 28-year-old James W. Jolley, from Delray Beach, Florida, John L. Barringer, aged 27, from Tucson, Arizona, and George S. Bezak, of Newcastle, Pennsylvania – he was to be diverted over 3,000 miles back in the direction from which he had just come; back to Palomares.

Jon Lindbergh's key role in the H-bomb hunt would be to assist in the co-ordination of the activities of the three undersea craft, Alvin, Aluminaut and Cubmarine.

He was an obvious choice for this important task. Although he held a private pilot's licence he had decided not to follow in his father's famed footsteps. He became interested in marine life when he was a teenager. On the West Coast he enthusiastically pursued his hobby of skin-diving and exploring underwater caves. During three years service with the U.S. Navy he had been attached to the Underwater Demolition Team (UDT). He came out as a Lieutenant (Junior Grade) and was now a Lieutenant-Commander in the Naval Reserve.

In Madrid thirty six hours later, on the afternoon of Wednesday, February 2, Jon Lindbergh went aboard a U.S. Air Force transport plane, together with Mr Duke, General Donovan and several embassy officials, and flew to San Javier.

He was whisked off by Army helicopter to the beach-head and then taken out by landing craft to the guided missile heavy cruiser U.S.S. Boston (CAG-1), which had arrived three days earlier to relieve the destroyer U.S.S. Macdonough, as flagship for Task Force 65.

Admiral Ellis, Commander of the Sixth Fleet, had just concluded a visit to the salvage operation area and in the plotting room of the 16,700-ton warship – the world's first guided missile cruiser and armed with Terrier missiles – each contact located by the search units was being carefully marked with coloured pins on an array of charts.

The Boston, apart from its missiles and conventional armament, including 8-inch, 5-inch and 3-inch guns, was fitted with extensive electronic equipment, and the communications requirements of the Task Force, both within the force and to other commands, were handled by the ship's radio and signal personnel. The cruiser was also used to provide the logistic and technical help so necessary to the other ships and units supporting the salvage operation.

Admiral Guest welcomed the young oceanic expert aboard and later gave him a detailed briefing – prior to the imminent arrival of the submersibles – on all aspects of the sea hunt.

His briefing revealed that 67 metallic objects had so far been detected either by the frogmen, SCUBA and 'hard hat' divers or the armada of eleven warships now engaged in the hunt using high resolution sonar, OBSS, underwater television and the Sea Scanner. Among these 67 were the two mysterious objects that could be parts of the elusive bomb, although there were no positive signs of confirmation. Admiral Guest had instructed that samples of seawater should be taken in the search zone every eight hours, but so far, not even the slightest trace of radio-activity or contamination had been found in the sea.

Final identification of the objects would have to wait until the subs went into action. Already the conning tower of the Alvin had safely arrived at Rota with the C-141, but the hull section in the second plane had been further delayed in the United States because of bad weather.

Meanwhile, dozens of little red and orange marker buoys bobbed on the waves and local fishermen from Aguilas and Garrucha had been ordered not to cast their nets in the zone, while those from Villaricos had been instructed not to sail their boats. Instead, the fishermen had been hired by the Air Force to assist in the land search.

The Soviet fishing trawler, reported to be inching its way in the direction of Palomares from its usual position outside Spanish territorial waters off Rota, had not yet appeared but Admiral Guest was kept informed of its exact position. The possibility that Russian deep-diving submarines might be oper-ating in the area was also being investigated.

Ashore, four colossal earth moving machines began the systematic destruction of tomato, bean and onion crops in a 37-acre area of fields. Their giant wheels crushed the plants, and the teeth of the mechanical monsters dug hungrily into the parched soil, ripping up the withered vegetables by their roots. Huge piles of vines and rotten fruit were set alight and blazed like funeral pyres, representing thousands of pounds worth of ruined crops. Spanish scientists from the Nuclear Energy Com-mission sifted freshly tilled ground, making tests with geiger counters and alpha scintillation meters.

Mr Duke assured Senor Gonzalez, the acting mayor of Palomares, that there was no danger to public health, and that the U.S. government would continue to pay out full compensa-tion for all losses and damage.

'When we saw American airmen and soldiers eating tomatoes and oranges in the restricted area we knew there was nothing to fear,' said the mayor, who himself had several acres of tomatoes, oranges, onions and string beans behind his tiny white stucco house. 'We want everyone to get a fair compensation, and we are glad that some of the claims have already been paid. We can't, of course, allow a few unscrupulous people to take advantage of the situation.'

The ambassador revealed that ejection seats, galley equipment, part of the B-52's wing, and various parts of the plane had been recovered from the shallow waters near the beach.

'Our mission is to leave Spain as we found it before the accident,' he declared. 'The massive search operation could probably last at least another month.

'The crash happened on the day of Saint Anton, the patron saint of Palomares. This reinforces the belief of the villagers that it was a miracle when no one was killed by the flaming debris.'

More and more tents continued to mushroom from the sand at 'Campamento Wilson', as the 'Broken Arrow' land force swelled to 700. Each day the Air Force was pumping in 50,000 gallons of water to dampen down the dusty tracks and for drinking and washing purposes. The search itself was further extended over an area of 15 square miles to include the sparsely-inhabited villages of El Arteal, and Las Herrerias, in the Almanzora river-bed region, and Las Cupillas, La Mukria and Los Lobos, in the foothills of the Sierra del Castillarico range.

In the nearby town of Huercal Overa, on the N.340 highway towards Murcia, General Wilson spoke to 300 heads of families who had assembled at the local cinema. He expressed the satisfaction of the U.S. government for the 'magnificent comportment of the residents of this area during a time of stress.' He, too, repeated the assurance that there was no health hazard. But one of the scientists of the Nuclear Energy Commission warned that although the nuclear devices were unarmed and there was no danger that the missing one could explode, radioactivity might be released if there was any accidental damage to its casing. He thought the radioactivity would not be in quantities that would be harmful to health, however.

Although many of the villagers still felt some resentment at the American intrusion into their lives, tension was slowly easing. Such so that the teenagers even composed a pop song entitled 'La Bomba Ye-Ye!'

'Oh, you don't want to know, Ye-Ye,
That the bomb's going to explode, Ye-Ye,
And a pocket sub is coming to see,
Just where it might be.
But we won't give it to you, Ye-Ye,
'Cos we're going to hide it again soon, Ye-Ye!'

*　　*　　*

Three unarmed nuclear bombs had landed around Palomares
– but where? It was pointless asking the Americans, who were
not even prepared to admit that any bombs existed. As a news-
paperman it was my job to find out and I set off towards
'Campamento Wilson'. But this time, instead of turning towards
the beach-head encampment, I steered straight ahead, in the
direction of Palomares. The car was kicking up such a trail of
dust that I felt sure it would be spotted, but I was able to drive
undetected right on to the sandy beach. The American camp
was then over a mile to the right.

Out in the bay the U.S.S. Boston rode its anchor together
with the three other warships, each slowly turning their bows to
face a stiffening breeze which whipped up white caps on the
waves. Strung out along the horizon were more patrolling ships
in a protective arc.

Suddenly I heard the roar of an approaching engine and
noticed tell-tale clouds of dust being churned up along the
track I had taken through the tomato fields. I could just make
out a grey Land Rover bumping its way to the beach where I
was standing. That's it, I thought, the police have spotted me.

But I was wrong. The Land Rover lurched to a halt, its wheels
sinking slightly in the fine yellow sand, and a man wearing grey
corduroy trousers, white open-necked shirt, black waistcost and
a beret alighted from the driving seat, followed by two young
boys of about six and eight, yelling excitedly.

'Buenos dias, senor,' said the man extending his hand in a
friendly greeting. 'I have brought my sons to show them the
big ships.'

Farmer Jose Portillo was also to supply me in the next ten
minutes with some of the missing pieces in the jig-saw puzzle of
what was happening at Palomares.

'You know where the bombs fell?' he asked, casually. I shook my head. 'Well, you see that old fort over there, senor,' he continued, directing my gaze towards the Moorish fort where I had witnessed the strange activities of the men in masks. 'Look at that orange flag flying alongside. That marks where the first bomb landed.

'I went to that spot and saw the bomb before the Americans dug it out and took it away. It was an awesome looking weapon, and had buried itself almost completely in a big crater. It was silver in colour and tilted at an angle.'

His description was identical to that given previously by the architect, Senor Puig. But where had the other bombs dropped? The sun-bronzed farmer wheeled left and pointed back towards the right-hand edge of the village.

'Look carefully at the skyline,' he instructed. 'There, can you see it? The other orange flag.' Sure enough, another bright orange pennant fluttered above the rise and near to a square building.

'That one fell near one of the village's electric transformers,' he explained solemnly. 'I have tried to go there but the immediate area has been sealed off and only men in white protective suits and masks are allowed to enter.

'From here you will not be able to see the spot where the third bomb fell. That is on the other side, beyond Palomares, up in the hills near the village cemetery. But I can tell you there is another orange flag flying there, too.

'There are several of these masked men working up there as well. I was not allowed near enough to see the bomb.'

Senor Portillo paused for a moment to reflect. 'You know, senor, it is truly a miracle that those bombs did not explode and that no one was injured.'

His two sons, who were now throwing pebbles into the sea and then chasing each other round the beach, had been among the terrified schoolchildren huddled at their desks when the flaming wreckage had plunged down on that fateful morning.

'It is very strange, senor, but if you look again you will notice that the three bombs fell roughly in a line, each about a mile apart. It seems that the fourth bomb is in the sea.'

Senor Portillo stooped down and beckoned me to do the same. Shading his eyes against the glare of the sun he pointed out to sea, almost directly in front of the fort.

'You see it?' he inquired, and I could just distinguish some red and orange marker buoys about a mile offshore. There was also a tiny U.S. Navy craft, with about six people aboard, circling the spot.

'No, not the boat or the buoys,' he added, 'the other flag?'

I strained my eyes for several seconds in the direction he was still pointing. There seemed to be at least twenty buoys. Then, against the blue horizon, I spotted what he was trying to show me.

Near where the boat was circling was a larger buoy supporting a long post which swayed in the wind and from which another large orange flag billowed.

'That's it! That's where the missing bomb might be lying, underneath that buoy!' he declared.

The longer I stared the more I could see. Frogmen were splashing in the water around the little boat, but they were not diving. They were securing a network of buoys. Was Senor Portillo's assessment correct? The orange flag at sea was in a line with the other three on land, and the distance between each was about a mile. Obviously something important nestled on the seabed many fathoms below that bobbing marker buoy.

Was that where the fourth deadly hydrogen bomb had landed? Had they found it, at last?

CHAPTER SIX

THE INCESSANT rumble of the homeward-bound city traffic penetrated through the shuttered windows. It was already dark, and there was an air of tension inside the spacious neon-lit office.

Back in Madrid, at his glass-topped desk in front of the draped Stars and Stripes sat Mr Duke, the ambassador, deep in thought. Trouble was brewing in the Spanish capital as a result of the nuclear bomber crash, coupled with the recent controversial decision of President Johnson to resume bombing raids on North Vietnam after the brief truce with the Vietcong.

In that instant the shrill, insistent ringing of the telephone interrupted the uneasy silence.

Mr Duke leaned forward to grasp the receiver. Before he had time to speak, a gruff voice at the other end of the line warned menacingly: 'A time bomb has been planted inside the building and will explode within an hour.'

There was a click and the line went dead. Mr Duke, a worried frown creasing his brow, leaned back in his chair. Another anonymous caller had delivered his threat. Should he be taken seriously, or was he just a crank?

The ambassador was taking no chances. Already, since his return from Palomares, he had received other warnings that the embassy in the fashionable Calle Serrano – Madrid's Bond Street or Fifth Avenue – was about to be blown up. In addition, there had been no less than five telephone calls threatening bomb attacks against himself and his family. And earlier that morning, Friday, February 4, he had received in the post a mysterious package. When security officers cautiously unwrapped the brown paper all they found was an empty Coca Cola bottle, a bar of black chocolate and a grubby note which demanded 'Free Viet Nam.'

Mr Duke picked up the house phone and requested the U.S. Marines on guard duties in the entrance lobby below to organise once again a routine search of the building.

Outside the tall, concrete building, the green-painted metal gates had been closed and padlocked. The embassy was surrounded by over 100 armed Spanish police.

It was the night of the expected demonstration, and even as Mr Duke conferred with his aides about the latest bomb threat, thousands of left-wing students, labourers and white-collar workers were converging on the building in a bid to force the closure of the American military bases in Spain.

Hundreds more grey-uniformed police reinforcements from the crack Policia Armada – nicknamed the Grey Plague – patrolled the nearby streets or sat in riot jeeps waiting.

Thousands of leaflets had been distributed by underground Communist factions urging the mass protest.

With police stationed at every corner it appeared that the scheduled demonstration might fizzle out. But, suddenly, as if from nowhere, thousands of students formed a large group in front of a church across the street from the embassy and began chanting anti-American slogans. '

'Away with the bases!' 'Yankees no, Yankees go!' 'Johnson is a murderer!'

They marched forward, holding aloft burning newspapers, to parade in front of the embassy railings. When they refused to disperse, the police, unsheathing their long leather batons, charged into the mob.

In the screaming confusion, demonstrators were knocked over and trampled on, and one policeman who was clubbing a student was set upon, savagely attacked and beaten unconscious.

Late-night shoppers and passers-by were caught up in the melee as the demonstrators panicked and fled in face of the repeated, flailing charges of the police. Some students and workers tried to re-form into smaller groups but each time were broken up.

Traffic snarled to a halt in the chaos and cars were damaged. Several arrests were made, and among those detained were two of the ringleaders who were in possession of 1,600 leaflets calling for the demonstration. These two youths, Luis Garrido Domingo and Fernando Arevalo Penalba, were, three months later, sentenced to two years' imprisonment and six months' respectively for 'spreading illegal propaganda.'

The street battlefield slowly cleared and no time bomb was found in the embassy. But Communist-inspired troublemakers were already planning further demonstrations to step up their illegal activities in an attempt to force a wedge between American and Spanish relations.

Just four days later, Russia was to launch a bitter attack on the United States during a disarmament conference on Western policies in Geneva, Switzerland.

Soviet disarmament negotiator Semyon K. Tsarapkin said Western Europe 'is sitting on a nuclear volcano' because of these policies.

'Recently three bombs fell on the coast of Spain,' he cited. 'It was only a fortunate stroke of luck which saved the Spanish population in this area from catastrophe. This shows how urgent nuclear disarmament is, and a nuclear non-proliferation treaty is the first step.'

Angrily American delegate William C. Foster jumped to his feet and said the accident 'demonstrated just the opposite to what the Soviet representative claims.'

He added: 'There was an accidental collision between a bomber and a tanker. Both planes crashed and some crew members died. Such accidents are extremely rare. No nuclear explosion occurred because the controls, designed to prevent such explosions in such accidents, performed as intended.'

*   *   *

The hull of the Alvin finally arrived at Rota but as it had to be assembled and undergo test dives before being ferried aboard a U.S. Navy landing ship dock to Palomares I was able to make another sortie into the tomato fields.

This time I was joined by Reginald Peck, correspondent of the *Daily Telegraph* who had arrived from Bonn, and Patrick Chapman, from the London office of the *Express*.

Together we drove down the same track, through the fields and on to the beach. Here we parked the car and trudged along the soft sand round the headland towards the Moorish fort where the orange flag was still flying.

We managed to get to within 50 yards of the fort. All that we could see was the square-shaped khaki tent and massed aerials of the Decca electronic master station which was facing out towards the cruising warships. We returned to the car and drove back towards Palomares. At the bottom of a rise we parked the car under a fig tree and walked up a pebble-strewn pathway. The two farmhouses at the top of the rise appeared to be deserted. There· was a strange stillness in the warm air as we followed a footpath around the deserted farmhouses. Below, to our right, were the fields with the red flags dotted among the green plants. But directly in front, about 100 yards away and near the post from which the now-tattered orange flag was flapping, was a scene like something out of a science fiction film.

At least 30 masked men, in white protective suits and rubber-taped boots, were busily engaged shovelling up the dry, hard-packed earth. Already a sizeable chunk of the hillock where they worked had been flattened out by a yellow bulldozer parked nearby.

Six lorries, each with a wooden crate clamped on the back, were lined up in a row in front of where the masked men toiled. The flaps at the back of the crates had been opened. Masked airmen, in muddy fatigues, stood a few yards away where a red water wagon was spraying the ground. Some of them carried geiger counters and alpha scintillation meters, which they used frequently to test the brown soil. As the masked men sweated and shovelled up the earth it was being hosed down and then heaped into the crates in the lorries. Hundreds of tons of earth had obviously been dug up and transported away secretly.

Even more astonishing was the weird activity among the flattened alfalfa grass beyond the flagpost. Here a white sheet had been strung up around the lip of a crater which was at least 20 feet in diameter. Inside could be seen the crouching figures of half-a-dozen more masked men, probably scientists, who appeared to be collecting soil samples and sealing them inside plastic bags. The depth of the crater was impossible to establish and there was no visible sign of a bomb.

Incredibly, all this was still happening, 22 days after the crash.

The ground had been tidily raked and was still being sprayed when, later, we turned to walk away. But two suspicious guards came panting up the slope and ordered us to stop. We meekly handed over our credentials, but they were not satisfied. One of them said he was going to fetch a senior officer while the other silently kept guard over us.

Nearly ten minutes later we heard the footsteps of the returning Guardia Civil and his companion. We fully expected to see a Spanish policeman accompanying him, but it was an American Air Force sergeant.

His name 'Haley' was emblazoned on a blue flash stitched over the left breast pocket of his fatigues. Slung casually under his chin was a blue face mask and we noticed that the sideburns under his black beret had been covered with white tape and so had all the pockets and a tear on his fatigues.

'Gentlemen, I must advise you to get out of here immediately,' said the bespectacled sergeant, coming straight to the point. 'This area is highly radioactive!'

We looked, and felt, stunned. 'Is there any danger?'

Sergeant Haley, pointing a gloved hand back towards the orange marker flag, explained grimly: 'That is where one of the four bombs landed.

'The impact caused the conventional TNT detonating charge to explode and this resulted in the bomb's casing being blown apart. The nuclear content from the core was consequently scattered about on the ground and we are still searching for radioactive pieces.'

So Doctor Bethe, the scientist, had been right in his assumption that one of the bomb's might have cracked open! The villagers of Palomares had been potentially exposed to the effects of radiation from scattered plutonium!

The sergeant warned: 'The danger lies in the wind which isn't helping at all. The nuclear particles carried in dust have been spread over a considerable area of the fields down there.

'This dust can't harm your skin, but it can be dangerous if you swallow or breathe it. That's why we are all having to wear these protective surgical masks.'

The sergeant carefully scrutinised our documents. 'I suggest that if you want any more information you go to the camp by the beach. You must leave here at once. This is a restricted zone.'

Escorted by one of the Spanish guards we returned to the car and drove hastily from the area feeling a certain amount of alarm at Sergeant Haley's dramatic disclosures.

One mystery still remained unsolved, however. Where were the lorries taking their contaminated cargo?

The answer was to be provided the following day. Army and Navy helicopters from their pads by the beach were making frequent excusions into the hills behind the village.

And from their car, as they approached 'Campamento Wilson', three newsmen – Dutch reporter Joost de Ruiter, of *De Telegraaf*, Italian photographer Marco Schiavo, of the magazine *Oggi*, and cameraman Tito del Amo who, like his brother Andre, was with UPI – spotted the helicopters on their curious missions.

They decided to follow them to their destination. They managed to drive their car along a track for almost a mile and then carried on up into the hills on foot.

All the time the helicopters, their rotor blades thwacking noisily, appeared overhead like angry wasps. It took the three almost an hour to reach the place where the helicopters had disappeared from view, over the brow of a hill. They also had to run a gauntlet of Guardia Civiles. But, finally, they made it. And below them, in a tiny valley, they observed yet another amazing scene.

A convoy of six lorries, laden with the crates we had seen the day before, was winding its way into the hills along a heavily-dampened track. A red water wagon was parked, waiting for the lorries to arrive, along with more of the masked men in white. Huge pits had been dug in the ground, and a tunnel gouged into a hillside. The lorries drew up alongside the pits. Then the masked men proceeded to measure the radiation count of the contaminated earth inside the crates with their electronic meters.

Afterwards, they began shovelling tons of soil from the crates into the pits while it was continuously hosed down with water.

The whole burying operation took almost half-an-hour. Then while the earth was still being sprayed, the masked drivers climbed back into the cabs of their lorries to return and fetch the next radioactive load.

On the hilltop the frequent click of a camera shutter recorded the incident before the three uninvited observers faced the ordeal of a nightmarish descent back to their car.

*   *   *

The American and Spanish governments were extremely angry – and justifiably – at some of the wild reports being published throughout the world about Palomares; the Americans because of the anti-U.S. feelings that were being aroused and the distorted propaganda instigated by the Russians; the Spaniards because of the immeasurable harm likely to be inflicted on the season's tourist trade.

Two examples of blatant irresponsibility illustrate why their anger was aroused to boiling point.

A Milan magazine published a picture showing the ruins of the abandoned mine near 'Campamento Wilson' and, in the caption, referred to the aftermath and desolation which had been caused 'by an H-bomb explosion.'

Worse still was the 'exclusive' splash story published in Australia in the *Sydney Sun* on Tuesday, February 8. 'The TNT detonator in a U.S. hydrogen bomb exploded yesterday spreading deadly radioactive rays over a wide area near the little Spanish town of Palomares,' claimed the report. 'Killer rays were released when an explosion ripped open the casing of the hydrogen bomb. Thousands of people have fled from the area which has been sealed off by emergency troops rushed to Palomares by giant transport planes. Work has already begun on decontaminating the countryside where the explosion occurred and U.S. troops are digging for radioactive fragments. The transport planes which brought them to Palomares are being used to fly hundred of tons of "live" soil out to sea to be dumped.'

Someone, somewhere along the line between Palomares and Sydney, had married fiction to fact and repercussions were bound to follow. An immediate denial of this text was issued at Torrejon declaring it was 'ridiculous and absurd', and the Spanish Ministry of Information and Tourism described the report as 'completely phoney.'

Britain at the time was in the throes of preparing for a second General Election within two years, but the newspapers, after their initial disinterest in the nuclear bomber crash, began to pose a number of intriguing questions.

The non-sensational, influential and so-called Top People's newspaper, *The Times,* stated informatively in an editorial: 'In times of relatively good relations with Russia it is often forgotten that the United States still maintains a vast fleet of bombers in constant readiness around the world. Only during crises, or when something goes wrong (which is extraordinarily seldom), do they make their presence felt. Then they are often judged in rather emotional terms.

'The question that is bound to be asked is how necessary the flights are. The Strategic Air Command developed its present shape during the 1950's, when America's strategic missiles were few and vulnerable and Russia's air defences were relatively easy to penetrate. It has become less useful since Russian air defences developed, and since the United States developed the almost invulnerable Minuteman and Polaris missiles. Mr McNamara has, indeed, fought hard – against the combined pressures of the Air Force and the aircraft industry – to cut down the S.A.C. and to avoid embarking on expensive new projects to prolong the life of the manned strategic bomber.

'Even he, however, told Congress recently that although the United States had more than enough missiles to destroy both Russia and China simultaneously bombers would provide an extra safeguard and force the Soviet Union to spend extra money on providing a defensive system. A certain amount of bomber capacity would be maintained "indefinitely", but much of it would be taken over . . .

'Mr McNamara is as aware as anyone that the lumbering giants of the type that crashed in Spain have largely outlived their usefulness. The power that bears the main responsibility for defending the West cannot switch policies and weapons overnight.'

The *Sunday Citizen*, meanwhile, was demanding the answers to five questions about the crash.

A front page article said the following questions 'should be answered – and promptly' about the lost bomb:

'Is it radioactive?'

'Can it blow up?'

'Is the recovery operation solely a security – not a danger – cloak?'

'Is the same sort of bomb flown in the same sort of plane liable to crash in the same way off Brighton, Blackpool, Cannes, Ostend as well as off Spain's holiday coasts?'

'Why can't we be told?'

The newspaper added: 'It is a gross error to underestimate

the ... insanity of this operation ... all southern Spain would be shattered if a nuclear bomb exploded.

'Conclusions to be drawn are either the bomb could go off, the U.S. wants to ensure that the Russians don't try to recover it secretly later, or there is real danger that the bomb's thick casing might corrode and its radioactivity spread to the shore. This is the most likely.'

The *Sunday Express,* however, in a page one article, answered two of the above questions. It said there was 'very little possibility of either a catastrophic explosion from an acknowledged unfused H-bomb, or serious risk from radiation if it was broken or shattered in its descent.' The paper added: 'The only possible reason remaining to cause the U.S. to mount such a vast security-conscious operation is that it fears another power might find the remaining H-bomb and learn its secrets.'

So controversy raged. Certainly, a similar accident involving a U.S. nuclear bomber could next occur in Britain. In London, a Member of Parliament said he would ask Prime Minister Harold Wilson to ban flights over Britain by any aircraft carrying nuclear weapons. The M.P., Mr William Hamilton (Labour, Fife West, Scotland), announced he would ask for an assurance that no overflights would be allowed with either armed or unarmed nuclear bombs 'in view of recent happenings off the Spanish coast.'

Another M.P., Mr John Brewis (Conservative, Galloway) said he was going to ask the Foreign Secretary, Mr Michael Stewart, in the House of Commons, what advice he would give British tourists intending to visit Spanish Mediterranean resorts 'in regard to radiation danger from the U.S. nuclear bomb.'

*　　*　　*

No one could help but admire – even if they did not have a clue what was going on – the slick execution of the 'Broken Arrow' operation.

It was the first time that such a nuclear accident had ever occurred in Europe, yet here was a gigantic task being undertaken with such smoothness and efficiency that it gave the impression that the men in charge were experienced hands at the job.

The Big Three responsible for the success or failure of 'Broken Arrow' were General Wilson, who masterminded various phases of the work to be done on land, General Arturo Montel Pouzet, who spearheaded the detachment of Spanish Air Force personnel, and Admiral Guest, aboard the cruiser Boston, who led the sea hunt.

With a phone link being established to Torrejon, General Wilson was eventually able to make direct contact with military chiefs at the Pentagon. Over 800 men were now assigned to the beach camp. Each one had a specific task to perform.

There were those responsible for the running of the camp, such as the cooks, the engineers, the electricians, the drivers and the entertainments officer who, apart from the regular film shows, arranged for a special bullfight for the troops in the sanded ring at nearby Vera.

There were those engaged in the hunt for plane wreckage and the missing bomb. Daily they would move off in batches of 100 to scour the fields, hedgerows, mountain slopes and barren land for miles around.

There were those damping down the dust. And there were those masked men in white, undertaking the decontamination of infected fields and digging up thousands of tons of contaminated soil.

At 'Campamento Wilson', men were busy with hammers, nails and saws constructing the huge crates into which the contaminated soil was to be shovelled. A large number of blue painted barrels had also appeared.

A centre had been established for a subsidiary task, named 'Operation No-Dust', which was a decontamination process and had Colonel Alton White, from Torrejon, in charge. A large white notice board had been put up alongside a tent, listing important instructions to be observed by airmen engaged in the work, which consisted of hosing down soil and wetting windrows, scraping off two inches of topsoil and loading it on to lorries. A warning to halt work, in the event of wind starting to churn up dust, was also displayed.

As well as the field hospital, a decontamination (or isolation) tent had been erected. Here, the airmen handling wreckage or engaged in the bomb search, had to undergo routine daily radiation tests, shower, and send their clothes to the laundry.

General Wilson had decided to rotate the men at the camp every 21 days as this was considered a hardship assignment. Before leaving, each man had to spend 12 hours in the isolation tent where urine specimens were taken to test for possible radiation exposure. The Air Force was taking no chances.

The fate of the thousands of tomatoes purchased by the Americans was more difficult to establish. Empty crates were often piled up on the beach. One of the most popular joking explanations was that they were being ferried out to the ships and then dumped overboard, the resulting 'sea' of tomato ketchup making it impossible for the submersibles, when they arrived, to detect the bomb. In fact, the tomatoes were devoured in such large quantities that sailors and airmen eventually became fed up with eating them.

In the fields, work was being stepped up and by Wednesday, February 9, a ban on the sale of crops was partially lifted. A number of farmers, whose land had been inside 'la zona contaminada' – the contaminated area – for over three weeks, were finally allowed to return to their fields. They were told they could now do what they wished with the crops which had been tested for radioactivity, and cleared.

Elsewhere in the countryside, hundreds of airmen with bamboo poles spread out and jabbed at the ground in the belief that the missing bomb might have buried itself on impact. One airman carried a pole topped by an animal's skull and a bright red scarf.

The masked men in the fields, where the red flags were still fluttering, yanked up tomato plants and piled them into waiting trucks. The blue, lumbering vehicles maintained a shuttle service to and from the fields, bumping off in the the direction of the next-door fishing village of Villaricos. The men rode atop of the heaps of twisted vines, dirt and rotten fruit.

In some fields the tomato plants were being burnt or fed into giant shredding machines. One mechanical device, orange-coloured and shaped like an anteater, buried its snout into the earth. As the motor whined, airmen wrapped excavated soil into huge plastic sheets, to be hauled away later. Tractors ploughed up the trampled earth in the stripped fields as water wagons sprayed the ground.

With more and more newsmen flooding into Palomares from

all over the world Spanish government authorities, alarmed by the erroneous reports, took stern action. Entry to 'Campamento Wilson' was barred to all except correspondents accredited by the Ministry of Information and Tourism.

This meant that many impatient journalists from abroad would have to apply to Madrid for credentials, a chore that would take at least two days. Many did not bother and based their stories on what they could see in the fields or out at sea.

Blanket security precautions still persisted. I was stopped by plain clothes men on so many occasions in so many different places that they must have got fed-up writing down my name. There were moments of pure farce – like the day when a car-load of journalists managed to get through the road blocks and drive into Villaricos.

The Americans had moved in to make their routine radio-activity tests. Before they set out with their geiger counters and electronic meters and donned their masks they were handing out bubble gum to children and stood puffing fat cigars in the main square. Along with Reginald Peck, Patrick Chapman and Roy Rutter, the *Daily Mirror* man from Paris, I managed to drive right past the throng of people to the local bar at the far end of the village. Undetected, so we thought.

Just offshore, U.S. Navy frogmen in black and yellow rubber suits were diving from a pontoon and stringing out red for danger corks to mark wreckage below. Further out was the orange flagged buoy underneath which the bomb was thought to be lying. It appeared much closer to the shore.

But as soon as we sat down at a table in the porch half-a-dozen security policemen converged warily on the bar from various directions. They eyed us suspiciously. We ignored their gaze, sipped our drinks and stole glances towards the frogmen. The six sleuths were hesitant. Were we spies? They sat down at the next table to make up their minds about tackling us. They watched us as we endeavoured to watch both them and the divers. After ten minutes of this watching cat-and-mouse game they pounced, demanded our credentials and finally ordered us out of the village. We finished our drinks first.

Attention now switched to the Polaris submarine base at Rota. At last, the 19,500-ton landing ship dock U.S.S. Plymouth Rock (LSD-29) had steamed slowly into the harbour after a choppy Atlantic crossing from Miami, Florida. Its precious cargo: the submersible, Aluminaut.

The tiny craft with its conning tower aft, diving propellor bang in the centre of the orange deck, and escape hatch and battery of lights, television cameras and port holes on its stubby nose, was stowed at the rear of the ship above the large 394-foot by 48-foot floodable deck from which small craft could be launched and recovered.

Instead of its usual role in amphibious assaults the Plymouth Rock – maximum speed 22 knots – would eventually provide support for the divers and ships of Task Force 65, and share the task of acting as a mother ship for the submersibles. It also carried its own miniature flotilla of seven landing craft, two 135-foot LCU's, two 75-foot LCM8's and three 56-foot LCM6's. These boats would be used for inter-ship transportation as well as platforms and debris recovery units by EOD/UDT divers. Its two revolving cranes would winch the submersibles from the deck into the sea.

Aboard the Plymouth Rock were the two Aluminaut pilots, Robert E. Serfass, aged 40, from San Diego, California, and Robert H. Canary, 48, from Miami.

The arrival of the Plymouth Rock coincided with the successful completion of test dives by the little, silver Alvin. It was proposed to ferry both subs to Palomares at the same time.

Naval technicians had worked through the night to prepare for the departure. The Alvin had been manoeuvred alongside the landing ship dock, steel cables hooked on, and then it had been slowly hoisted up to a cradle where it had been clamped on the deck.

So, by mid-day on Wednesday, February 9, all was set for the final lap in the 3,000-miles quest of the Aluminaut and Alvin, to recover a hydrogen bomb. With an optimistic toot on its foghorn the Plymouth Rock sailed off in a southerly direction, hugging the Atlantic coastline, then going through the Straits of Gibraltar past the cloud-shrouded Rock, towards the search area.

Offshore from Palomares, a curtain of 11 warships, with the cruiser Boston anchored in the middle, had spread out in a shielding arc. A vast radar and sonar network extended from Aguilas in the north to almost Almeria in the south.

Every precaution seemed to have been taken to ensure that any operation launched by a foreign power would not stand a chance of penetrating the area without being detected.

U.S. Navy officials dismissed as 'inconceivable' the chances of a Soviet submarine sneaking through the net and stealing the bomb. Intruders would not be permitted within the 12-mile limit of Spanish territorial waters. However, it was admitted that an officially designated submarine exercise was taking place 25 miles northeast of Palomares, and, in addition, there was an explosives dumping zone 40 miles away.

The number of contacts located on the seabed had by now risen to over 100. Each one would have to be investigated and then retrieved.

Admiral Guest again studied the observations of the fisherman, Francisco Simo. From Aguilas, Senor Simo had been taken out by boat by a U.S. Navy officer and had pointed out the spot where he said he had seen the parachutes fall. The Americans had nagging doubts that he could be correct. First, the spot was not in the provisionally established zone of 'high probability.' This zone was a triangle, 20 miles from tip to base and 10 miles across, where scientists had calculated the nuclear device was most likely to have splashed down.

Second, Senor Simo had not taken a compass bearing of his boat's position on the morning of the accident. So how was he able to say the spot he was indicating was precisely the same one he had been at before? He had relied on his own uncanny skill as an experienced local fisherman to return to the spot without a single navigational aid. Was his sighting accurate? The admiral was not prepared to dismiss Senor Simo's account out of hand, despite the suspicions, and decided to play a hunch. Orders went out for the fisherman to be brought out to the flagship by helicopter so he could be questioned further. Then, if he could take the U.S. Navy back to the identical spot again, without a compass, the submersibles would be sent down to probe the murky depths where Simo indicated.

On the Thursday morning, the Plymouth Rock at last arrived, turned its bows towards the shore and anchored alongside the landing ship dock Fort Snelling and the cruiser Boston.

Jon Lindbergh was taken across from the flagship to confer with Mr Rainnie, the chief pilot of the Alvin, and the crewmen of both subs which were being prepared for immediate lowering into the sea.

Ashore, lorries were carrying rocks and boulders to the beachhead, where a long jetty was under construction near the camp. Landing craft or even submarines would eventually be able to dock alongside, unload any debris they might recover and take shelter in any sudden squalls.

From the emergency headquarters in the cinema headquarters of the Spanish Nuclear Energy Commission, came the welcome and relief news that the danger from contamination was slight. Said and official: 'To produce in animals or persons any danger there would have to be radioactivity 50 times greater than that found in the area.'

Senor Gonzalez, the acting mayor, was told to explain to the villagers that the Americans were simply taking super precautions.

Late that Thursday afternoon, when everything seemed set for the Aluminaut and Alvin to start their searches the light suddenly faded. The blue sky turned an evil dark brown, and a terrifying wind swept down from the Sierra Lisbona mountains. This was the dreaded Mistral, a tropical and violent windstorm that strikes without warning.

Within seconds, 60 m.p.h. gusts ripped across the beach. Clouds of choking dust and sand reared up as though in a tornado. The subs disappeared from view as the clouds of dust curled and descended on them. Visibility was cut to no more than one yard.

The Mistral would undoubtedly be causing havoc to the vital 'Operation No-Dust', although thousands of tons of dust, almost certainly carrying alpha particles, was now being carried out to sea from around Palomares. It was fortunate that the wind gusted seawards and not inland. Even so, the dust storm was a prelude to more disasters.

CHAPTER SEVEN

A T 7.26 p.m. on Saturday, February 12, a giant C-124 Cargomaster aircraft began its roll down the runway at Moron Air Base, near Seville. The aircraft, of the U.S. Military Airlift Command (MAC) and with eight airmen aboard, was on a routine transportation mission to the San Javier military airport, home of the Spanish Air Academy, with a load of two buses, trucks and camping equipment, destined for the search headquarters at Palomares.

Normally, the Cargomaster was attached to the Hunter Air Force Base, Savannah, Georgia, but it had been assigned first to Germany and then to Torrejon, after the crash of the nuclear bomber, to assist in the 'Broken Arrow' operation.

In Palomares, gale force Mistral winds continued to sweep the area and had paralysed the hunt at sea for the H-bomb. But conditions at Moron were perfect for flying. It was a clear night and the stars twinkled brightly. Only 66 minutes later the plane was due to touch down at San Javier, which was being used by the U.S. Air Force because it was the only place near Palomares with a runway long enough to take the big, cumbersome transport aircraft.

The navigator, Captain James P. Cisco, had plotted the route almost due east across southern Spain, over the ruggedly wild mountainous country between Cordoba, Jaen and Granada, and above the sinister, snow-capped Sierra Nevada range.

Fifteen minutes after take-off as the plane levelled at 10,000 feet and droned on through the night the pilot, Captain William Cornwell, radioed back to the Moron control tower. He reported that the weather was clear with broken low clouds and gusty surface winds.

That was his last message. All contact with the plane was then lost.

There was a possibility that the radio had packed up, but when

113

there was no sign of the aircraft at San Javier at the scheduled landing time of 8.32 p.m. the worst was feared.

Colonel James N. McFadden, the Commander of Moron base, who was at home with his wife and three sons, was immediately informed and a big ground and air search was ordered. Five hours later, with the hunt in full swing, it was officially announced at Torrejon that the plane was overdue.

The Cargomaster had almost certainly crashed in a snow-storm among the craggy peaks of the Sierra Nevada, but there was the slim chance that the eight aboard might have survived. They would have to be rescued quickly, however, before they froze to death.

Five hundred Guardia Civiles, in the province of Almeria, toiled up the sides of mountains in the freezing cold darkness, the beams of their flashlights trying to pick out any signs of scattered wreckage among the rocks, boulders and pine trees. Others struggled knee-deep in powdery snow drifts to scan the carpet of whiteness. No one in the many isolated villages nestling in the foothills had heard an explosion or seen the flames of a crashing plane that night.

At first light, U.S. Air Force rescue and spotter planes from Moron and Torrejon criss-crossed along the missing aircraft's route, in an effort to trace it. Silver-winged C-97's and C-54's swooped low towards the menacing, needle-sharp peaks of the tallest range in Spain. Observers strained their eyes through the cotton wool clouds down to the white slopes. Aerial photographs were taken, to be enlarged many times in an effort to detect even the slightest sign of twisted metal. Bus loads of American airmen and G.I.s were rushed to the area and joined the weary Spanish rural police, now red-eyed through lack of sleep.

All day the grim search went on – but they found no trace of the Cargomaster. Hope faded of ever finding the eight airmen alive.

The search was called off that night but resumed at dawn. It was a few hours later that a lone Guardia Civil stumbled over a mangled lump of wreckage, partly buried in the snow. Almost simultaneously a tiny search plane circled overhead. The Spaniard explored higher up the mountainside and spotted more lumps of jagged metal protruding amidst snowdrifts. The fate of the Cargomaster had been finally discovered.

The site of the crash was at Spain's aptly-named Death Peak – the 11,600-foot Mount Mulhacen, the highest in the peninsular. Less than 16 months before, in October, 1964, a French airliner had slammed into the same mountain, killing all 80 people aboard.

Inevitably, from the Valdeinfierno – Vale of Hell – alongside Mulhacen the shocked Guardia Civil sent back his message to rescuers still scouring below for signs of the Cargomaster: 'No survivors.'

The plane had clearly been caught in the terrible turbulence around Death Peak and the eight airmen who had been busily engaged with their tasks were killed outright in a second of crunched, exploding impact between steel and icy rock.

A bizarre trail of wreckage littered the flanks of the mountain. No part of the plane, with its nose-loading doors, vehicle ramps, rear cargo hatch with elevating loading and auxiliary floor for double loading, was distinguishable. Only the tail section remained and this tilted grotesquely in the snow. The buses and trucks aboard had disintegrated, although a number of wheels had rolled down through the snow and propped themselves against pine trees.

It was another 24 hours before rescue parties could struggle through clinging snow, tempestuous gusts of wind and swirling low clouds, to start bringing down the bodies of the eight air-men – Captain Cornwell and Captain Cisco, co-pilot First Lieutenant John F. Archheaux, flight engineers Staff Sergeant Donald G. Gallitzin and Sergeant James W. Thompson, the load master Staff Sergeant Ronald W. Hickman, and crew members Staff Sergeant Charles R. Anderson and Airman 2nd Class Kenneth C. Young.

The rescuers had to make their ascent first by donkey and then on foot to reach the spot where the wreckage had been strewn over a three mile area. It was a macabre scene, identical to the French airliner disaster, with the bodies of the crewmen torn beyond recognition.

The crash of the Cargomaster now brought the bomb-loss incident death-toll to fifteen.

*　　*　　*

The big fishing expedition for an H-bomb was at a standstill. High winds continued to gust around the search fleet at Palomares.

Nothing was going right for the Americans. Prospects of the submersibles going into early action had been shattered. And the tiny Alvin, secured to a buoy, was being lashed and pounded so roughly by the angry sea that it was in danger of being severely damaged or even toppled over and sunk.

Aboard the Plymouth Rock, Mr Rainnie, who had anxiously watched the tiny craft's ordeal, gave instructions for an attempt to be made to bring the Alvin back to the safety of the landing ship dock. A small craft put out with six sailors aboard and was cruelly buffeted in the mountainous seas. It took almost an hour for the boat to reach the Alvin which it then circled as it tried to pull alongside. It was a hopeless task. If the boat ventured too close it ensured being smashed against the hull of the sub.

There was no sign of the wind abating. Drastic action was called for. One of the sailors volunteered to try and leap on to the deck of the Alvin to try and secure a tow line. A rope was tied round his waist and when the boat neared the violently rolling submersible he stood up, poised to jump. Salty spray was being blown in his face but he still managed to straddle the ten feet between the two vessels. His hands clawed at the silver deck for something to grip as he was hurled half back into the sea by a sudden wave. Somehow he managed to cling on and then pull himself up on to the deck so that he could lash himself with his rope to the conning tower.

It was a brave effort. Within five minutes, the tow line had been secured, the Alvin freed from its anchor buoy, and the long haul back to the landing ship dock was underway.

The larger Aluminaut rode out the storm less alarmingly from its anchored position, 100 yards from the Alvin. But for 90 minutes, the five men in the boat and the sixth, who had now disappeared down in the conning tower to steer the Alvin, battled to reach the protection of the Plymouth Rock. On seven different occasions attempts to enter the well deck were baulked by the high seas. Each time the boat towing the Alvin, about 15 yards behind, had to turn out to sea and circle round for another bid to slip into the shelter of the U-shaped dock during a lull in the squalls. Eventually, at the eighth try, the bid was successful.

The Alvin, still reeling from the pounding it had taken, was dragged into the rear of the ship from where it was later hoisted back on to its cradle on the deck above. Mr Rainnie and his team of scientists then had to set to work examining the delicate equipment inside the tiny sub to locate any damage that might have been caused.

Meanwhile, yet another warship had steamed in to join Task Force 65 – the U.S.S. Tringa (ASR-16), a sister ship of the submarine rescue vessel Petrel, and commanded by Lieutenant-Commander R. E. Lanphear.

The 2,000-ton Tringa was equipped with underwater television and, like the Petrel, also carried sonar for detecting objects on the seabed and an underwater telephone for communications with submarines or other undersea craft. Both these ships carried an extensive amount of special submarine rescue and salvage gear, such as rescue bells and decompression chambers.

The mission of these two ships would be primarily as diving platforms and equipment vessels for the Navy's specially-trained deep-sea diving teams. Their Master and First and Second class divers were highly trained for both deep and shallow water diving. Both ships carried a large number of bottles of oxygen and helium-oxygen for diving requirements. The helium-oxygen mixture would be used generally at depths of 200 feet or more to reduce the affects of nitrogen narcosis. Divers from the Tringa and Petrel would be used to aid in the identification and recovery of underwater objects at the salvage sites.

The third submersible, the tiny Cubmarine, 22 feet long and weighing 6,350 pounds, was also on its way to the scene. It had been flown across to Rota from the United States and was now being prepared for shipment to Palomares.

The Mistral, which had dropped during the night, sprung up again the following day and once more created havoc as dust spiralled in the air. Phone communications, even from the American camp, were disrupted as lines were ripped down and telegraph poles snapped in the 65 m.p.h. gusts.

Finally, after almost 48 hours, the winds subsided, the sea calmed, and Aluminaut pilots Robert Serfass and Robert Canary prepared to make the first exploratory dive.

A launch took them out to the anchor buoy where the circular hull of the sub was inspected and found to be none the worse for wear after its battering by the waves. The pilots boarded the Aluminaut as the launch drew alongside, opened the escape hatch on the tiny conning tower construction at the rear, and eased themselves, feet first, below.

For almost an hour they sat crouched inside the craft, thoroughly testing all the controls and checking the mass of gauges, switches and dials.

Then, gliding away from the anchorage, the Aluminaut headed out to sea past the cruiser Boston, where sailors lined the deck rails to watch. A few minutes later it slipped, amid hissing spray, below the waves.

The submarine rescue ship Petrel steamed behind at about 3 knots, its course indicating the direction in which the Aluminaut was moving over 200 feet down.

Visually, through the portholes and even when using the television camera, the two pilots could only see as far as the nose of their vessel and the stabilising fins. The bad weather had stirred up the seabed so much that normally clear water was clouded with swirling sand and masses of black seaweed. They would not find the bomb that day. An hour later the Aluminaut, whose pilots had maintained telephone contact underwater with the Petrel's 41-year-old Commanding Officer, Lieutenant Max A. Harrell, of Charleston, Carolina, slowly surfaced.

The Alvin was temporarily out of action before it had even made its first dive. Minor repairs were needed after its storm battering and the batteries had to be charged up. The sub also had to be switched to the second landing ship dock, the Fort Snelling, to enable the Plymouth Rock to set off back to Rota to collect the Cubmarine.

It was not until Tuesday, February 15, when the dockship with the third submersible aboard returned, that the Alvin was seen to make its first descent – probing the depths offshore from Villaricos around the area of the bobbing orange marker buoys.

One of its first tasks was to investigate the two mysterious objects located about 2,000 feet underneath these buoys. The silt had now settled back on to the seabed so the pilots, Valentine Wilson and Marvin McCamis, were able to have a bird's eye view in the inky depths with the aid of the powerful spotlights. If the two objects were parts of the bomb, which might have cracked open on impact, emitting plutonium, then they would have to be hoisted up quickly.

Aboard the flagship Boston, Admiral Guest, in his operations room, tensely awaited the radioed alert 'Instrument Panel.' These were the code words to be used when an important find was made on the ocean floor. They did not come that day. The two objects were, in fact, lumps of ordinary plane wreckage. The elusive H-bomb was probably lodged elsewhere on the seabed.

*　　*　　*

The Americans now faced a formidable task. Scores of underwater valleys, gorges and mountains would have to be explored within the triangle of the 'high probability' search zone. It would take months, perhaps years, to find the H-bomb. To say it would be like searching for a needle in a haystack was an exaggeration. It would be far worse than that!

Admiral Guest had other problems. The electronically-equipped Russian trawler had, at last, arrived to spy on the sea hunt, and had anchored only a mile outside the Spanish territorial limit.

The embarrassed U.S. Navy refused, officially, to acknowledge its presence. From the trawler's position outside the territorial limits, there was nothing the Americans could do except inwardly fume at the cheek of the Russians and attempt to jam the intruder's radio, radar and underwater scanning equipment.

Further embarrassment came from reports claiming that the U.S. Air Force had dropped a dummy nuclear bomb over Palomares from the same height and position where the B-52 accident had occurred. They had lost that bomb, too!

*　　*　　*

President Lyndon Baines Johnson was undoubtedly in a spot as a result of the B-52 crash.

Fate had played a strangely cruel trick. Here he was trying to curb the spread of nuclear weapons in the world, and right at the crucial moment America had lost an H-bomb in Europe.

Who can, on reflection, really blame the Defence Department from keeping its mouth shut about the whole, miserable affair? This was chronic irony.

The President, however, had to hide his embarrassment when, in a message to Congress on Tuesday, February 15, he said: 'I have committed my administration to the task of persuading the non-nuclear countries that it is neither in the interests of their security, nor of world peace, to develop nuclear weapons.'

Johnson went on to note that 'under the increasing pressure of the nuclear threat' arms control and disarmament had been taken up in 1965 at the first meeting in five years of the United Nations Disarmament Commission, at the 17-Nation Disarmament Committee meeting in Geneva, at the full session of the U.N. General Assembly, and in confidential diplomatic talks.

Indeed, the President himself had transmitted to the Geneva meeting a seven-point programme to halt the nuclear arms race and 'instructed our negotiators to walk the extra mile necessary to insure that the weapons of war submit to man's need for peace.'

Added Johnson: 'I reaffirm my belief that it is possible through reason and through patient effort to translate the world's common interest in survival into concrete acts of restraint and accommodation between the nations.'

Whether the non-nuclear countries would heed Johnson's pleas would remain to be seen.

But America's dropped political clanger – in the shape of the missing hydrogen bomb – would not be forgotten easily. Certainly, Russia meant to cash in fully on the incident with more preposterous propaganda swipes at the U.S.

The Kremlin's new accusations came the following day and were contained in a note handed over in Moscow by Foreign Minister Andrei Gromyko to Mr Foy Kohler, the U.S. ambassador to the Soviet Union.

The charges were not revealed, however, until 24 hours later at the Geneva disarmament conference. Russia's point-blank accusation was that America had contaminated the high seas as a result of the nuclear bomber crash.

In an aide memoire, which caught Western delegations completely by surprise, Russia charged that the United States had violated international law, the international convention on the high seas, and the 1963 Nuclear Test Ban accord signed by Washington, London and Moscow.

An immediate halt to all flights of bombers carrying nuclear weapons outside national waters was demanded.

'The accident resulted in the loss of nuclear bombs hundreds of times more powerful than the atomic bombs dropped on Hiroshima and Nagaski,' claimed the aide memoire. 'At least one detonating device exploded, causing danger of radioactive contamination. This danger is now hovering over a densely populated area.'

The aide memoire was delivered to the conference by the Soviet negotiator Comrade Tsarapkin, who nine days before had fired the first anti-U.S. tirade.

Tsarapkin had been expected to devote his speech to the issue of nuclear non-proliferation – a subject on which Canada and the United States were also scheduled to speak.

Instead, he produced the controversial aide memoire and asked for it to be made an official conference document.

'The accident was a flagrant contradiction of established principles and regulations of international law and also against the 1963 ban on nuclear tests in the air, on the ground and underwater,' it alleged.

'Now the American nuclear weapons have contaminated the southern coast of Spain and adjoining waters. The contamination is limited not only to the coastal waters but is spreading to the high seas.

'We see in this a violation of the convention on the high seas which was ratified by the United States in 1958.'

Russia warned there would be similar accidents if flights of bombers carrying nuclear weapons were allowed to continue.

'The Soviet government has time and time again warned of the danger of such flights,' the aide memoire went on. 'The United States did not heed these warnings and the flights are continuing. We must stop the flights of planes carrying atomic and hydrogen bombs outside national borders. The Soviet Union expects an immediate stop to such flights.'

Later that Thursday, details of the note handed by Gromyko to Mr Kohler were disclosed in Moscow. Its theme was almost identical to the tongue-in-the-cheek accusations made in Geneva.

Referring to the 1963 Nuclear Test Ban it said: 'The most important purpose of this treaty was to prevent radioactive contamination of the atmosphere, outer space and water of our planet. The crash subjected to radioactive contamination the south coast of Spain and the sea around it.'

Gromyko's note did not, of course, hint that the Russians considered the crash at Palomares an excuse to rip up the treaty. Extraction of the maximum propaganda out of the disaster was the only motive.

Mr Kohler immediately hit back declaring that the note contained 'many false allegations.' He stressed that his acceptance of the note should not be interpreted as acceptance in any sense of the Soviet charges. 'I accepted it only because it contained allegations of violations of international agreements by the United States to which the U.S. government would wish to reply.'

The government certainly did wish to reply. And less than nine hours later the United States rejected the Russian accusations. Mr Robert J. McCloskey, the State Department Press Officer, said the U.S. Air Force in Spain had acknowledged that unarmed nuclear weapons were aboard the B-52. Asked whether it was correct that U.S. completely denied the Soviet charges he replied: 'Yes, that is right.'

There was still, however, no official U.S. acknowledgment that one of the bombs was still missing even a month after the crash.

The following day in Madrid the Spanish government bolstered the American rejection of the charges by announcing there had been no infringement of any international treaty because of the crash. It was repeated that there had been no release of radioactivity on land or in the sea.

And Senor Iribarne, the Minister of Information and Tourism, pointed out after a cabinet meeting that U.S. and Spanish forces in Palomares 'eat vegetables, fruit and fish from that region and go swimming on the beach.'

But the row continued to fester and boil. Four days later, back in Geneva at the disarmament conference, Czechoslovakia's delegate Zedenek Cernik made the now-standard Communist attack against America because of the loss of the nuclear bomb. His charges then went deeper – accusing America of considering nuclear sharing in N.A.T.O. more important than a nuclear non-proliferation treaty. He adopted the Communist line that a non-proliferation treaty was impossible if the West went ahead with nuclear sharing in any form within the Western alliance. A non-dissemination pact, he said, must prevent both direct and indirect proliferation of nuclear weapons. Cernik claimed the

Soviet draft treaty contained no loopholes while President Johnson's proposed programme would permit indirect proliferation in the form of nuclear sharing in N.A.T.O.

Political 'fallout' from the crash, meanwhile, rained down all over the world.

In the Philippines, the foreign minister called for a revision of an agreement that gave the U.S. right to use bases there for nuclear bombers and nuclear powered ships.

In Bonn, the West German parliament was assured by Herr Gerhard Stoltenberg, Minister of Scientific Affairs, that food shipments from Spain would be closely checked for radioactivity.

In Holland, pacifist Socialist A. J. Bruggeman called for a ban on planes carrying nuclear bombs over the country. But Defence Minister, Piet J. D. de Jong, said such a restriction would harm N.A.T.O.'s defence in an 'inadmissible way.'

In London, the Labour government also refused to ban nuclear-armed planes from flying over Britain. 'No new factor has emerged as a result of the recent crash in Spain which would justify any change in the existing arrangements whereby under strict precautions certain flights of this kind are carried out over the United Kingdom,' announced Mr George Brown, the Deputy Premier, in the packed House of Commons. In answer to questions from Left-wing Socialist Mr William Hamilton, he said it was essential for security reasons not to divulge general information about the nuclear overflights. Another Left-winger, Mr Hugh Jenkins (Labour, Putney) demanded: 'Franco has belatedly given the Spanish people immunity from this risk. Are you not prepared to do the same for the British people?' Amid hoots of derisive laughter, Mr Brown retorted: 'There are many ways in which I have no desire to follow General Franco.' And, responding to Mr Brewis – the Tory who asked Mr Michael Stewart what advice he would give British tourists intending to visit Spanish Mediterranean resorts – a statement on behalf of the Foreign Secretary said holidaymakers could safely lay plans to bask and bathe on this coast.

Finally, ten days after Gromyko had handed his note to Mr Kohler and when still smarting from the Russian charges, America officially denied the allegations for the second time of violating the test ban treaty. On this occasion Mr Davis E.

Boster, Counsellor for Political Affairs at the U.S. embassy in Moscow, delivered a sharply-worded reply to the Soviet Foreign Ministry:

'The government of the U.S.S.R. must be aware – or could easily have ascertained – that no nuclear weapon test, no nuclear explosion of any kind, and no radioactive pollution of the sea were involved in the unfortunate accident over the coast of Spain.'

And to the Russian demand for a nuclear flight ban beyond national borders America firmly declared: 'It is common knowledge that flights of U.S. military aircraft are carried out with the agreement of nations of the free world and for the express purpose of reinforcing their collective security against the threat posed by the huge nuclear forces of the Soviet Union, including its many bomber aircraft.

'Our policies and practices, designed to meet this nuclear threat, have been adopted only after the most careful assessment of security requirements and after provisions of necessary safeguards.

'It is not surprising that the government of the U.S.S.R. is opposed to military security measures undertaken in defence against the threat of its armed power, or that it should attempt to limit or reduce such defence.'

The punch-line of the note said it was a matter of 'deep regret' that Russia should 'distort' the meaning of international treaties for propaganda purposes.

*   *   *

The sea was as smooth as a sheet of glass, the sun magnifying its deep blueness.

A thousand yards offshore, five U.S. Navy ships sat squat and motionless on an invisible swell while little craft chugged busily to and fro on their assigned tasks. On the horizon the dark, masted shapes of more warships could be seen prowling the sea, oily black smoke curling from their funnels.

It was perfect weather for the underwater quest, and all three submersibles were in action.

Task Force 65 was able, for the first time, to employ all the sophisticated equipment and devices which had been assembled in the hunt for the elusive bomb.

Scouring the depths up to 130 feet were the frogmen. Up to 200 feet – the MK-6 divers and the Sea Scanner. Up to 400 feet – hard-hat divers, the four minesweepers of Mine Division Eighty-Four with the Pinnacle towing the Ocean Bottom Scanning Sonar 'magic eye', and the Cubmarine with a robot grappling arm positioned under its snout. Beyond 400 feet – OBSS, underwater television and the Alvin and Aluminaut.

Several more ships had arrived to join the Space Age armada, among them the oceanographic research vessel U.S.N.S. Mizar (T-AGOR-11) with a crew of 11 officers, 29 men and 18 scientists.

The 3,300-ton Mizar, with its strange coffin-like structures on the centre deck, carried an impressive collection of underwater tracking equipment (UTE), including side-looking sonar, underwater television cameras and still-photo cameras. These gadgets were mounted on a 'fish' sled and towed over the search area to acquire both a visual and an acoustic picture of what lay hidden on the seabed below.

To stream out and recover this fish sled the Mizar had three special winches, one of which carried three miles of 30,000-pound breaking-strength armoured signal cable. The TV picture and sonar finds were relayed, through the signal cable, to the scientists aboard the vessel where a record and navigational plot was made of all contacts. Extensive film developing equipment was also available on the ship.

Once a contact had been located the Mizar was able to direct any of the submersibles to the object for attachment of a lifting line, and the main winch on the ship was then capable of lifting it – up to five tons in weight – to the surface.

Another recruit to the Task Force was the 1,675-ton fleet tug, U.S.S. Luiseno (ATF-156). This ship carried on board a decompression chamber for deepdiving operations and was also equipped with a fathometer for determining water depth, a heavy duty lifting boom, and a towing winch. A number of qualified divers were included in the crew and their job was to investigate and string out buoys above objects detected by sonar.

The Luiseno's normal function was to act as a towing ship but at Palomares its ten-ton boom played a vital part in the salvage operations.

The offshore frogmen, during one of their shoulder-to-shoulder explorations of the ocean floor, discovered another large section of the B-52's wing half-buried in ooze. Lieutenant-Commander Moody, in charge of the divers, realised his men could not possibly haul such a large chunk of debris to the surface. He contacted Lieutenant-Commander E. E. Wheat, commander of the Luiseno, and the boom was prepared to attempt the big lift.

It took the rubber-suited divers, working in shift relays, almost a day to secure lines to the wing section which, in fact, weighed almost ten tons. Then the tug's boom was swung out over the water about 30 feet and inch by inch the mangled metal was hauled up from its resting place in the seabed sludge.

The Luiseno's towing abilities were also being put to full use. Two lighters were loaded up with recovered and non-radioactive debris from the dump on the beach, and these craft were then towed by the tug along the Mediterranean coast and almost 100 miles out into the Atlantic, where the wreckage was dumped overboard.

Another key vessel was the U.S.S. Hoist (ARS-40), a 1,900-ton salvage ship equipped with two hoisting booms, one capable of lifting objects weighing ten tons, and one of 20-ton capacity. The Hoist, commanded by 42-year-old Lieutenant Commander Paul Kane, of Holyoke, Massachusetts, was in addition fitted with standard Navy communications gear and minor maintenance facilities. Its mission was to recover aircraft debris from the seabed offshore from Palomares and Villaricos. With the assistance of divers or, in deeper water, the subs, lines were fastened to objects to be recovered and they were then pulled to the surface by the ship's powerful booms and winches.

A destroyer tender, the U.S.S. Cascade (AD-16) steamed to Palomares from its normal support duties with the Atlantic Fleet to undertake its new chore as 'doctor' of the Task Force. On board, Captain L. K. Worthing and his skilled crew would provide day and night on-the-spot repairs for all units. The Cascade, at 16,000 tons almost as big as the flagship Boston, was outfitted with extensive machine shop, woodworking, welding and light manufacturing equipment. The ship's capability for repairing equipment and its proud boast of being able to manufacture any essential parts, enhanced maximum efficiency in all aspects of the search and salvage operation. The Navy ships involved, as well as the civilian-operated undersea craft and gadgets, relied wholly upon the support facilities of the Cascade at all times.

Meanwhile, the owners of the Aluminaut – Reynolds – sent over from Miami the 250-ton M/V Privateer, a support and tracking ship for the sub.

The Privateer, formerly the U.S. Navy submarine chaser U.S.S. McMinnville (PCS-1401), was equipped with the lastest radar, Loran navigation, and radio communications gear. In addition, the tiny vessel – maximum speed 14 knots – carried a fathometer indicating depths down to 900 feet, and a precision depth recorder capable of measuring down to 24,000 feet.

The ship, with eleven officers and men, plus quarters for an Aluminaut crew of six, was able to maintain excellent underwater telephone contact with the pilots of the submersible within a 12,000 yards range. Also aboard was an auxiliary diesel generator for charging the Aluminaut's batteries, a high pressure air compressor, and adequate space for servicing instrumentation and photography in the spacious scientific laboratory.

The primary mission of this vessel was to provide logistic and maintenance support for the Aluminaut and, in some instances, the Privateer could be used to control the sub like a robot while it was engaged in scanning the seabed.

On Monday, February 21, Mine Division Eighty-Four was relieved and the OBSS dismantled aboard the Pinnacle for installation on another minesweeper.

The four relief minesweepers, attached to Mine Division Eighty-Five, were similarly equipped with high-resolution sonar for hunting underwater mines and detecting objects on the ocean floor.

These four were the U.S.S. Ability (MSO-519) under the command of Lieutenant-Commander T. B. Potter, Junior; the U.S.S. Rival (MSO-468) commanded by Lieutenant-Commander C. R. Smith; U.S.S. Salute (MSO-470), Lieutenant-Commander J. M. Fitts, and U.S.S. Notable (MSO-460), Lieutenant-Commander G. W. Broun.

While each of the commanders was immediately summoned aboard the Boston for a briefing session with Admiral Guest, their minesweepers were being outfitted with Decca navigation equipment to link up with the master station set up on the cliffside by the Moorish fort, where one of the H-bombs fell.

This equipment would enable the minesweepers to determine within a few feet their geographic location and thus be able to search a specified area with assurance that no part of the ocean floor had been overlooked. Pinpoint accuracy of each contact would be essential in order to return again to the same location to investigate further or for one of the salvage ships to attempt recovery.

Initially, the minesweepers would have to fully and accurately sweep assigned areas within the zone of 'high probability', using their sonar, and locating and buoying all positive contacts.

So the United States had now assembled the most impressive array of equipment and skilled staff of oceanographic advisors, scientists and technicians in the world.

From this point the hunt for an H-bomb would proceed into deeper, darker and more dangerous waters.

*   *   *

If the sea search showed signs of hotting up, then operation 'Broken Arrow' on land was feverish by comparison.

The build-up of more troops in 'Campamento Wilson' only reinforced the belief that the Americans didn't really know where their missing bomb was and that it could perhaps have fallen on land after all.

There was also the distinct fear that it might have cracked open on impact. And, in Toronto, Canada, a leading U.S. nuclear physicist, Doctor Ralph E. Lapp, who helped to develop the atomic bomb in the wartime Manhattan project, warned that 'dirty bombs' with plenty of fall-out were usually carried aboard the B-52's. This was a feasible explanation for all the digging, spraying and decontamination efforts of almost 1,000 men.

It was significant, too, that General Wilson had detached helicopters along the coast past Mojacar as far as Carboneras, the fishing village from where the young British holidaymaker Eddie Fowlie had taken a snapshot of the bomber's sky collision. Airmen and G.I.s were being driven there by the busload to scour the barren foothills of the Sierra Cabrera.

If the bomb had fallen in this arid region of spiky cacti plants it was at least 15 miles from where the other three warheads had tumbled around Palomares. Theoretically it was quite possible

A B-52 bomber being refueled in the air by a KC-135 tanker.

Fatigue-clad U.S. airmen comb a dried-up riverbed, the Rio Almanzora, near Palomares, with
bamboo poles, geiger counters and alpha scintillation meters, for the missing H-bombs.

Villagers of Palomares with their crop of tomatoes declared "untouchable" immediately after H-bombs fell.

The "surgically cleaned" fields of Palomares after U.S. mammoth
clean-up operations.

Landing craft 1492—seamen's washing hanging from a line—waits on Palomares beach to ferry out contaminated earth barrels. There are 1,200 lined up on the beach.

The Aluminaut submersible.

Official photograph U.S.N.

Alvin submersible.

Official photograph U

OCEAN SEARCH

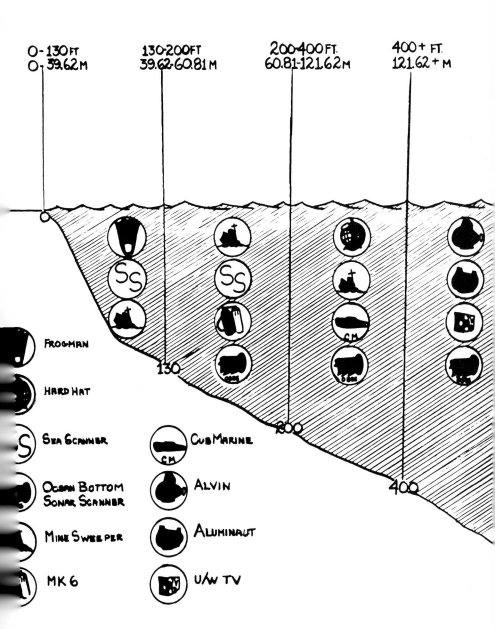

The Ocean Search—showing depths at which divers and equipment operated.

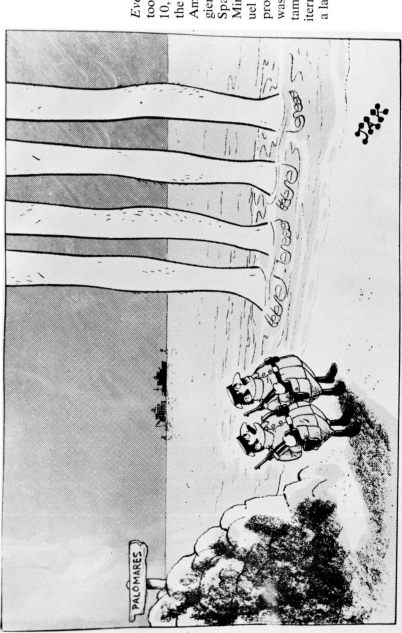

Evening Standard cartoonist JAK (March 10, 1966) decided that the swim by American Ambassador, Mr. Angier Biddle Duke, and Spanish Information Minister, Señor Manuel Fraga Iribarne—to prove to tourists there was no danger of contamination in the Mediterranean—was worth a laugh!

"Which one is the American ambassador?"

London Express Service

PALOMARES

The H-bomb is seen underwater as it is being hauled 2,850 feet to the surface. The transponder (foreground) was used by the submersibles, Alvin and Aluminaut, in order to relocate the contact on each dive in preparation for the recovery operation. The pinger (white object on parachute) emitted an acoustic signal to assist CURV (Cable-controlled Underwater Research Vehicle) in relocating the weapon in order to attach lifting lines.

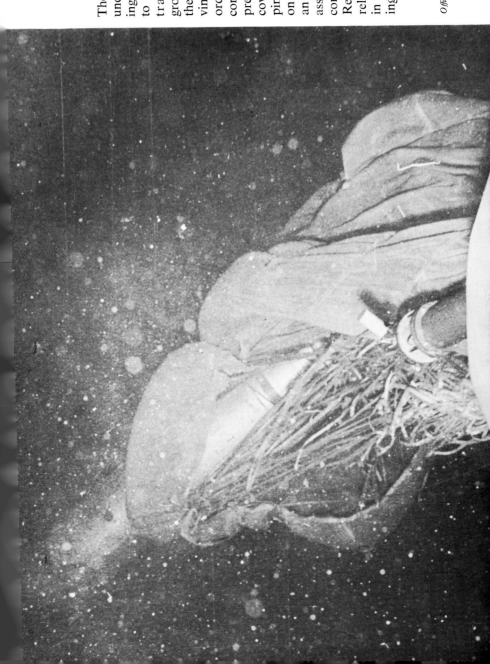

Official photograph U.S.N.

Fisherman Francisco Simo aboard his boat, Manuele Orts Simo, at spot where he stood and watched aerial collision.

Some wreckage of the two planes on beachhead dump alongside Campamento Wilson. In background a water wagon being used to spray and hose down possible radioactive materials.

Official photograph U.S.N.

On board the Petrel, Major General Wilson and Rear Admiral Guest examine the dented bomb after its recovery. The robot vessel CURV is in the background.

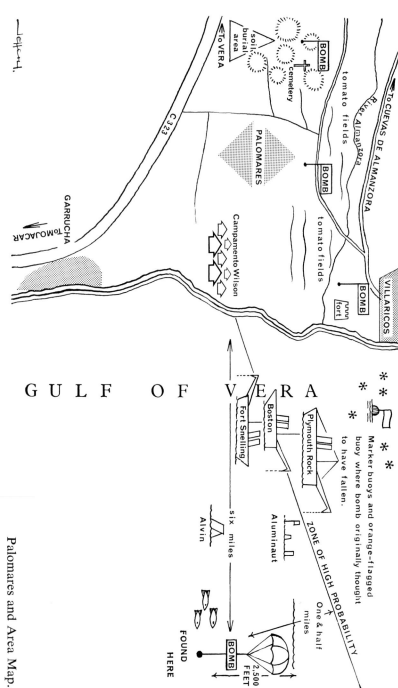

Palomares and Area Map.

Official photograph U.S.A.F.

in the confusion and panic following the B-52 mid-air disaster that there had been time to jettison properly only one of the bombs. The three that had plunged down near the village had been blown by the force of explosions from the bomb bay of the blazing aircraft. The fourth, however, attached to a parachute – H-bombs are normally dropped in this way to allow the planes time to get clear from the resulting nuclear blast – drifted slowly down from about 30,000 feet. But where had it landed? On the day of the crash there had been some air turbulence and it was difficult to calculate if a parachute with such a lethal cargo would have been carried inland or out to sea.

In any case General Wilson was convinced that a long, tough task lay ahead in finding the warhead.

And signs of permanency came to the beach-head encampment when convoys of lorries started to deliver bricks for an enclosed mess room to be built and with wooden floors being put down in most of the tent sleeping quarters.

In the tomato fields the cleaning-up process went on relentlessly. The vines were being systematically cut down, two inches of topsoil being scraped off the surface of all plots marked with the red flags, and the earth sprayed and then ploughed.

To some extent the villagers of Palomares had stopped worrying and were learning to live with the bomb.

The third bomb had landed in the hills behind the cemetery, and when I discovered where it was I found that its TNT detonator had also exploded on impact. That was why so much digging had gone on for so many weeks after the actual crash! Plutonium had obviously been scattered over a large area which, fortunately, was barren and isolated in the hills.

The chance of the missing fourth bomb having similarly cracked open was clearly a frightening possibility.

CHAPTER EIGHT

LUDICROUS. That, in one word, described the veil of official secrecy that still shrouded details of the crash as the big hunt entered its seventh weary week. The joint policy adopted by both Washington and Madrid to hush up the 'Broken Arrow' operation at Palomares was wearing irritably thin.

Officially, what the world knew *was* there – namely, the bomb – was not there. Officially, what had been lost was not missing. And, officially, what was nuclear armament was not an H-bomb.

As Colonel Young so confusingly put it: 'If you think we have found what you think we are looking for . . .' An exasperated pause, then: 'Think what you like! But don't think it's the truth.'

It was so absurdly obvious that a drastic re-think of policy was now becoming necessary. America would have to hide its embarrassment and counter the ridiculing Russian propaganda by 'telling all.' Spain would have to stop worrying about possible repercussions on its tourist traffic. Enough harm had already been caused by indiscreet silence.

And so, on Tuesday, March 1, came the first official admission that a nuclear bomb had indeed been lost.

It came from Senor Otero de Navascues, President and Director General of the Spanish Nuclear Energy Commission – the man who had supervised the radioactivity tests among the villagers of Palomares. He revealed that the number of persons who were theoretically exposed to the effects of radiation from one of the bombs that apparently broke open, either on impact or when the TNT detonator exploded and cracked the casing, was about 2,000.

'There has not been a single case of contamination that has merited that definition in the Palomares district among 1,800 who have been examined,' he disclosed. 'Results of the tests for external contamination have been practically negative.' And the scientist branded certain local residents who allegedly claimed to have been subject to dangerous levels of contamination as

130

'individuals in search of some notoriety.'

He said there was no danger to the populace from radiation and that all vegetables, fruit, milk, fish, meat and poultry were perfectly safe to eat.

'But the problem remains,' he added, 'of the search for the fourth bomb, which, because it is extraordinarily modern, the Americans must retrieve.'

He explained that about 6,000 tons of contaminated dirt dug up from the fields and the areas where radioactive materials had been scattered would eventually be shipped back to the United States for closer scientific examination, to determine the effects of the radiation spilled around Palomares.

These shock revelations of the Spanish nuclear chief provoked the policy-makers in America to make rapid reversals of their no-information tactics. And the following day – 44 days after the B-52 disaster – the U.S. finally broke its long silence and admitted that a 'nuclear weapon' was *missing* in Spain.

A bigger bombshell than the confirmation of the loss itself was the official confession from Washington that *deadly nuclear materials had been sprayed over several acres of soil around Palomares when two of the falling bombs set off conventional TNT explosions*. After detonating on impact the bomb casings were split open, thus spewing radioactive fissionable materials over a small area, in which there were, fortunately, no humans at the time. Quantities of enriched uranium 235, and plutonium 239 – one of the most toxic materials known to man in which radioactivity, according to scientists, persists for 24,400 years – were shot on to the soil, creating a potentially dangerous situation.

Mr McCloskey, the State Department spokesman, read out a carefully worded communiqué which confirmed that the B-52 carried several unarmed nuclear weapons, one of which had not yet been recovered. 'The search is being pressed off the Spanish coast for the discovery of material carried by the two planes involved in the January 17 crash . . . and for fragments of wreckage which might furnish clues to the cause of the accident.'

The crash had resulted in some uranium and plutonium being scattered in the immediate vicinity of the points of impact. 'There was no nuclear explosion,' it was emphasised.

U.S. and Spanish scientists had conducted detailed laboratory tests in the Palomares area during the 44 days since the accident and had found no evidence of a health hazard. Painstaking daily tests of humans, animals and plants were still being made.

The communiqué noted specifically that local farm produce as well as fish and milk from the animals were all perfectly safe for human consumption, thus confirming what the Spanish nuclear chief had outlined the day before.

'Steps have been taken to ensure that the affected areas are thoroughly cleaned up and some soil and vegetation are being removed. These measures are part of a comprehensive programme to eliminate all chance of hazard, to set at rest unfounded fears and thus to restore normal life and livelihood to the people of Palomares.'

The poisoned earth would be shipped to the United States for scientific examination and eventual burial in a nuclear graveyard at the Atomic Energy Commission's Savannah River plant near Aiken, South Carolina.

Mr McCloskey agreed when questioned that hazards could not be entirely ruled out because of the lost bomb. 'Built-in safeguards have allowed the U.S. to handle, store and transport nuclear weapons for more than two decades without a nuclear detonation,' his communiqué concluded. 'Thorough safety rules and practices have been developed for dealing with any accident which might result in the spilling of nuclear material.'

Mr McCloskey, claiming that 'security reasons' had been the prime factor barring the U.S. from previously revealing that a nuclear bomb was at large, said it was not known if the lost warhead was intact or if it had also cracked open.

The hunt would continue 'indefinitely' – on land and at sea.

On the question of compensation for villagers he said the United States 'has made known its intentions to pay damages and some claims already have been paid.'

Despite the belated official communiqué, there were still isolated reports of villagers suffering ill-effects. An account in the usually reliable magazine *Newsweek* told of a local farmer who allegedly had stumbled across and accidentally kicked the remains of one of the shattered bombs, inhaling plutonium dust. It was asserted that the farmer had suffered clear, though initially moderate, effects from the inhalations.

However, it was a pleasant change to see America at last

facing up to facts – and revealing some of them. As a result of the communiqué, the conjecture of radioactive danger to the villagers of Palomares, waned considerably. Only one fear remained: that the lost bomb might lead to a boycott by summer visitors of the Costa del Sol and Levante coast. Action, not words, was called for to dispel this fear.

In Madrid, Mr Duke, re-affirming that there was no trace of radioactivity from the tests which were still being taken every eight hours at different depths in the sea, commented: 'Every day the American airmen and sailors are eating the locally caught fish, and taking dips in the sea. There is no danger.'

His own words gave him an idea for some 'action.' A phone call was made to the Ministry of Information and Tourism. Mr Duke then announced that a concise solution to the problem had been reached with Senor Iribarne, the minister. The excellent prospects of the area for tourism would be spotlighted and at the same time the fear of radiation would be dispelled.

'Senor Fraga and I will go swimming at Palomares,' said the ambassador, simply.

*   *   *

High winds buffeted back to Palomares, making the sea choppy and again paralysing the underwater probes as swirling mud made it more difficult to see than in the worst London or Los Angeles smogs.

It gave the three submersibles time off to re-charge their near-exhausted batteries and enabled the scientists to make minor repairs and routine checks on the delicate instruments. The U.S.N.S. Dutton completed the oceanographic survey of a 127-square-mile area on Thursday, March 3, reproduced new charts and then departed, two days later.

Generally, the sea hunt in the Gulf of Vera was progressing well. Altogether, more than 200 objects had been located by the high resolution sonar, the Deep Jeep, underwater television and other gadgets. Then, the subs, salvage ships, frogmen or SCUBA divers had moved in to recover some of these objects.

Chunks of fuselage, an electric stove, more ejection seats and a toilet had been hauled up from the seabed. But of the elusive bomb there was still no trace.

The Alvin had made more than 50 dives to explore valleys, chasms and treacherous mud slopes 1,500 feet beneath the waves. From the deck of the submarine rescue ship Petrel, Mr Rainnie, the surface controller, had directed the two pilots by sonar telephone on missions to search areas inaccessible to the SCUBA and hard-hat divers. Television pictures were flashed on to the closed circuit screens and the scanning sonar bleeped readings went both to the pilots, Valentine Wilson and Marvin McCamis, and to the ship above. The tiny Alvin hovered above each contact, its spotlights stabbing a beam through the murky depths. A steel claw attached underneath the circular observation porthole on the nose of the sub was then manipulated to try and secure lift lines. It was exhausting, eye-straining work, requiring maximum patience.

The Aluminaut concentrated its search in deeper waters, about six miles offshore. Its role at first had been restricted to detection and investigation of seabed objects. But, eventually, after emergency modifications at the General Electric plant in America, its robot grappling arms had been flown out to Spain. The steel pincers had been extensively used to pluck lumps of wreckage off the ocean floor or to lassoo bulkier objects for winching-up by cable.

The Cubmarine had been similarly employed, in shallower depths up to 600 feet. Jon Lindbergh, apart from assisting with the co-ordination of the activities of all three submersibles from the Boston, had made several dives in this craft. It was so small that it seemed hardly possible that two people could squeeze inside the Cubmarine through the twin escape hatches. Yet they did get in and from the tiny cockpit, the pilots made their observations through a dozen portholes clustered around the conning tower.

'I haven't done much really,' said the young undersea explorer, modestly. 'But I must admit it's fascinating down there –a silent but dangerous world. There are big underwater mountains and narrow valleys. The terrain is similar to the hills surrounding Palomares. The danger lies in trying to manoeuvre the submersibles on the seabed. One wrong turn by the pilots could result in disaster. Trying to locate a small bomb in such a vast wilderness is a colossal task. It might take years and even then the search might be unsuccessful because the underwater currents are constantly shifting the seabed and the bomb could be buried and lost for good. Already one of the craft might have dived near the weapon, without locating it, because it was hidden in the sand or mud. It will be a remarkable feat if that bomb is retrieved.'

Jon Lindbergh went on to tell how he had also been down twice in the Alvin. 'We scoured the seabed for about an hour during the first trip but did not spot a thing. The visibility was not too good, about six feet. Usually the waters off the coast of Palomares are much clearer – better than off the Pacific northwest coast where I used to swim – but on the day I went down here the sea was rough.

'The second time down in the Alvin, the sonar detected a metallic object half-buried in the mud of an underwater valley. I got quite excited thinking it might be the bomb. But a closer look proved that it was merely a small chunk of a plane's fuselage. This was buoyed and later winched to the surface.'

Meanwhile, U.S. Navy investigators had spent hours ashore, assisted by Spanish authorities, questioning all the fishermen of Villaricos, Garrucha, Aguilas and at the other tiny ports dotted along the coast. Anyone who had been at sea on the morning of the crash was quizzed.

'Did you observe anything unusual falling by parachute and splashing into the sea?' they were asked.

Only three boats had been in the immediate vicinity where parachutes had plunged into the Mediterranean, about six miles offshore.

One was the brown-painted fishing smack Agustin y Rosa, skippered by Senor Francisco Gomis. The second was the vessel Dorita, owned by Senor Bartolome Roldan. And the third, over a mile from the other two boats, was the Manuela Orts Simo, with Francisco Simo at the helm.

The three skippers and their crews were interviewed on a number of occasions by the investigators, in the hope that they might remember some apparently insignificant detail that would yield an important clue.

The fishermen had all been too busy racing to the rescue of the three B–52 survivors – Captain Wendorf, the pilot, First Lieutenant Rooney, the co-pilot, and Major Messinger, the third pilot – to plot on a chart exactly where the different parachutes had fallen.

'Two parachutes fell in the distance quite near Simo's boat,' explained Senor Gomis. 'But these were greyish in colour, not like the red and white striped parachutes of the men. There seemed to be objects of some sort suspended beneath them but I couldn't make out what they were.'

Added Senor Roldan: 'Yes, I saw those parachutes, too. But they were definitely not carrying survivors. It appeared to me that there were some boxes strapped beneath. Our first consideration was to try and pull the American airmen out of the water. One of them was entangled in the cords of his parachute and had to be freed. By the time they had been rescued the other parachutes had sunk. We all searched around for a while but then headed back to Aguilas because the Americans seemed to be in urgent need of medical attention.'

Senor Gomis and Senor Roldan had repeated their eyewitness accounts, patiently, many times. They had been flown by helicopter to the camp at Palomares and out over the sea, near to where they had been fishing. But neither was able to give an accurate bearing on the spot where these parachutes had splashed down.

Only Francisco Simo was able to do that. He had already led the Americans out to the spot once by memory and without the aid of navigational instruments or the compass. And the Americans had been sceptical. Surely no man – not even a Christopher Columbus – could remember an isolated spot in the middle of an ocean, with any degree of accuracy?

The U.S. Navy investigators had plotted Simo's spot on their charts and returned to their ships to continue the search in another area with their sophisticated underwater craft and devices.

Senor Simo, somewhat baffled by the attitude of the Americans in not despatching one of their subs to his spot and sending it down to investigate, went back to fishing on his creaking, 14-year-old boat. Each morning the Manuela Orts Simo chugged slowly out of the harbour at Aguilas, shortly before 4.0 a.m. Aboard were Francisco Simo's two brothers, Jose and Alfonso, and the crew members Lucio, Domingo, El Belele, Jesus and Charqueles.

They had been warned not to fish near the zone where the

big bomb hunt was going on, but frequently, as they cast their nets, they could sea the outline on the horizon of patrolling warships several miles to the south west. It seemed a waste of time to them.

Selling their daily catch – an average of about 180 pounds of gambas – had become increasingly difficult, with the widespread fears of contamination. The large shrimps which Senor Simo normally sold for 100 pesetas a kilo – 12 shillings for just over two pounds – had dropped in price by more than a third.

Some evenings, when they returned at 7.30 p.m. with their catch, there had been a U.S. Navy officer waiting on the quayside to question Simo and his crew.

'I must have had at least 25 conversations with the Americans,' he recalled later. 'I repeated over and over again the details of what I had seen on the morning of the crash. They showed me charts and asked me to pinpoint the spot where I had seen the large parachute, and its strange cargo, sink.

'Then, senor, they suggested I should take them out to sea again.'

So once more he directed the Americans to the spot, without the aid of instruments and relying for his bearings on the position of the sun and the mountain range near the shore five miles away.

The Americans were amazed. He led them to within 500 yards of the spot he had pointed out on his first trip. But Simo was not surprised at his accuracy. 'I know these waters like the back of my hand,' he said, with a shrug of the shoulders. 'I think I could almost guide you here blindfolded.'

Again the position was marked down on the charts. Again the Americans went back to their ships. The depth was probably over 2,000 feet so either the Aluminaut or Alvin would have to make a probe at the spot. Surprisingly, they were still not sent to dive.

Instead, one of the minesweepers, using its sensitive sonar, circled the spot but made no positive contact with any object that might have been lying on the seabed.

This did not help Simo's case very much, but he was persistently questioned again when it was disclosed in the Spanish Press that an unidentified fisherman from Aguilas had caught *a mysterious black box* in his nets.

The 'caja negra', according to the daily newspaper *Ya*, had been attached to a parachute and was believed to contain secret documents or equipment from the B–52 bomber.

So, it seemed true that the lost bomb might not be the only objective of the hunt, and that there were some strange black boxes missing as well. Boxes vital to Western security, boxes to transmit false signals and upset enemy radar defences, boxes to work out flight routes and target details if an attack was ordered, boxes which should have been automatically destroyed in the crash – highly classified boxes containing equipment which now had to be found, at all costs.

What *Ya* did not know was the identity of that fisherman who had found the black box. But it was, in fact, Francisco Simo.

'The black box and its parachute were recovered some weeks after the crash,' he revealed, later. 'Although we were not allowed to fish within the zone of the search we went back to the area where the large parachutes had fallen – the one with the light blue box attached to it, and the other with what appeared to be a tall man suspended beneath. This was almost two miles outside the search-zone and we often cast our nets there. Then, one afternoon, as we hauled up the nets, we could hardly drag one of them back on to the deck because there was something heavy lodged in it.

'We struggled to lift it. Through the clear waters we could just make out a square metallic object caught in the netting.

'It certainly was not a bomb, senor, but we were very excited. There seemed to be something resembling a parachute attached to this little box.

'Unfortunately, our nets, especially small for catching gambas, were not strong enough to hold this box. We pulled hard and without warning the netting ripped and the black box slowly sank out of sight.'

Senor Simo reported what had happened to the Spanish authorities at the harbour offices in Aguilas when he returned that night. The Americans were immediately informed.

'I was advised not to talk to anyone about the unusual catch while the hunt was still going on,' he explained. 'I had no idea what we had caught in our nets, but it must have been important because the next day the U.S. Navy went out to the spot with the chart bearings I had given them and apparently retrieved this object from the seabed.'

There was no real doubt that the U.S. Army, Navy and Air Force were looking for, and recovering, other top secret equipment from the scattered wreckage of the B–52, on land and from the sea. This was confirmed by the fact that photographers were being barred at 'Campamento Wilson' from taking close-up pictures of the wreckage-dump because 'classified objects' had been deposited there for radioactivity tests, scientific examination, and eventual transportation back to the disaster investigators at Torrejon.

Another news report from London suggested that the Americans were also searching for the trigger device of the bombs: a key, attached to a chain around the pilot's neck, which had been lost during Captain Wendorf's parachute descent. This key, it was claimed, could arm the nuclear bombs when it was plugged electronically into the warheads.

If this was the case anyone finding both the key and the lost weapon would be able to detonate the H–bomb.

It was at this intriguing stage of the hunt for the 'Big Catch' that the burning curiosity of the skipper of the Russian spy trawler was aroused to such a peak that he decided to pull up anchor.

For nearly a fortnight – as the Defence Department was later to confirm in Washington – the trawler had been strategically anchored at a distance of 10 to 13 miles from the zone, keeping watch. Now, the skipper slowly steamed his vessel closer and closer, to within five, then four, and then a mere three miles of the recovery operation.

Aboard the flagship Boston, Admiral Guest had been immediately informed of this dramatic new development.

The Soviet trawler had no right to venture inside Spanish territorial waters. But if U.S. Navy warships were alerted to intercept and screen off the unwelcome spy, an international incident might be provoked. The Americans wisely held their hands. After a few hours, the Soviet skipper, apparently satisfied with what little he had been able to observe or detect on his radar and sonar – and probably unnerved by his own daring – turned the trawler back.

An hour later, only a faint trail of smoke marked its position beyond the horizon where the trawler, heading towards the Straits of Gibraltar, had disappeared from sight.

* * *

With the United States finally admitting a nuclear weapon was astray, further political fall-out was inevitable. There was renewed criticism of the B–52 nuclear flights and their Western defensive role.

'Keeping B–52 bombers with a nuclear load always in the air is defended as a precaution so that Americans can never be taken by surprise,' said an editorial in the independent Left-wing British newspaper, the *Sun*. 'In periods of extreme cold war tension no doubt this is a justifiable precaution.

'But just now relations between Russia and America are relaxed. Does anyone believe that a nuclear war is round the corner? The nuclear patrols should be called off. However slight the risk of disaster, it should not be taken.'

Another line of criticism asked why the U.S. had taken six weeks to clear up suspicion, surmise and anxiety about the bombs that fell at Palomares.

'So far, it is claimed, no radioactive danger to health has been found. But why sealed lips for so long?' asked the *Sun*. 'Why such a ruthless security blanket over what had actually happened?'

In Moscow, the government newspaper *Izvestia* urged that the United Nations should take up the question of the B–52 crash and the lost bomb. Soviet writer, M. Mikhailov, calling the incident to the attention of Secretary-General U Thant, said the U.N. should deal with questions which posed a 'threat to universal peace and to international security.'

He added: 'Undoubtedly this present situation involving the crash is this kind of situation. This is the view of millions of peoples and many nations whose security and health are threatened by the fall of American H–bombs.'

In Paris, the evening newspaper *Le Monde* said the U.S. military, in launching such an enormous search for the lost weapon, tried not only to avoid a danger of contamination but also all chance, however little, of the 'thermonuclear secret' getting into other hands.

'In that, they shared one of the essential preoccupations of a whole sector of the U.S. administration: to prevent dissemination of nuclear or atomic arms outside the circle of the five great powers. This preoccupation is, it is known, shared by the Soviet and British governments and talks have been underway for the past month on this subject, in Geneva.'

The French editorial concluded: 'One wonders if it is really necessary for the United States, now that it commands close on 1,000 inter-continental rockets sheltered from attack in underground silos, and almost 40 Polaris-firing submarines assured of total immunity, to continue to fly aircraft armed with H-bombs around the world.

'As far as the mirage of our strike force is concerned it is to be hoped the military authorities have not lost any time ordering the necessary security measures.'

Back at the Geneva conference table the topic of nuclear non-proliferation was being swept aside as Comrade Tsarapkin, the Soviet delegate, again brought up the loss of the H–bomb in Spain to support his demand for the 'elimination of foreign military bases and withdrawal of foreign troops' from foreign territories.

He said America was using bases in South East Asia, Latin America, the Near and Middle East and Africa as 'jumping boards for aggression; a means of fighting the National Liberation Movement.'

The Russian accused: 'It is from these bases in South Vietnam, Thailand, Okinawa, etc., that the American aggression in Vietnam is perpetrated, and barbarous air attacks against the democratic republic of Vietnam and some regions of Laos are carried out. One third of American forces serve outside the United States.

'The U.S. ally, Britain, is not far behind in this field. More than half of British forces are stationed overseas in bases scattered over the world.'

Tsarapkin went on to call for the establishment of nuclear free zones, particularly in Central Europe, and a ban on the use of nuclear weapons. He turned down an American proposal to start nuclear disarmament by destroying a certain number of atomic weapons as 'having nothing in common with disarmament or with reducing the nuclear danger.'

In fact, America – red-faced at the H–bomb fiasco in Spain – and Russia appeared, on the surface, to have made very little progress at the 17-Nation conference towards a treaty banning any further spread of nuclear weapons, although there was always the chance of a compromise.

* * *

The object of my second trip to Palomares was to cover the 'swim-in' of the U.S. ambassador and the Spanish cabinet minister, and also to observe how the 'Broken Arrow' operation was progressing.

In the space of a fortnight 'Campamento Wilson' had undergone drastic changes. The bulldozed goat-track to Palomares had been flattened out even more and was practically a dual carriage highway. The Guardia Civiles, however, still patrolled the entrances to the camp meticulously checking credentials.

But once inside, the reception was frankly cordial. Gone was the brusque 'No Comment' greeting of the month before. Gone was the strict clamp-down on information, and gone, to a certain extent, was the secrecy surrounding the cleaning-up activities.

Information, previously suppressed, was now readily available. There was even the offer of a guided tour of the decontaminated zones on a Press bus. The Americans were falling over themselves to be helpful.

What a pity they had not been so co-operative before! The damage had already been done, and they had only themselves to blame for most of it.

Unfortunately, Colonel Young, who had painfully borne the brunt of the earlier no-information policy, had returned to Torrejon, prior to taking up a new appointment at the Pentagon where he had been assigned to work under Major General Ben LeBailly, Director of Information of the U.S. Air Force. His place at the camp had now been taken by his deputy, Major Moore.

The major, in regulation fatigues and with a blue silk scarf slung round his neck, had a less restricted task than his predecessor. He was able to talk. He explained that the number of troops at the beach-head, where almost 1,000 had at one time been encamped, was now considerably reduced. It was an indication that the long, dusty land search was being concluded, and that hopes of finding the bomb around Palomares were virtually nil.

Dozens of fields had been stripped of their tomato vines. The topsoil had been removed and the sun-parched earth hosed down before being ploughed. All round Palomares the blue tractors were still at work, the airmen-drivers were still wearing protective surgical masks, and the scientists were still making radioactivity tests in the areas which had been cleaned. But green flags had now replaced the tattered red ones in areas which had once been marked as contaminated zones.

The main batch of airmen still engaged in the hunt for the bomb were concentrating their efforts in the dried-up Almanzora riverbed.

From the top of the hill overlooking the riverbed it could be seen that at least 150 men were spread out in a line, with their bamboo poles, geiger counters, alpha scintillation meters and field telephones, walking shoulder to shoulder in the direction of the sea. Some of the men carried bright red or blue flags. These were to be placed in areas where radioactivity might be detected or where still unrecovered lumps of wreckage might be found.

It seemed remarkable that this sort of toothcomb operation was still going on, exactly 50 days after the crash.

If the bomb had fallen on that dry, hard riverbed, with its pebble and boulder littered surface, the impact would have caused the conventional TNT detonator to explode. Only tiny fragments of the warhead would be left. But the troops found no radioactive materials. In any case they had already scoured this same ground many times before.

Less than a mile away, peeping above the tufted alfalfa grass and the cactus plants, were the mastheads of the warships still anchored close to the beach.

Through binoculars the three midget submersibles, a vivid orange, silver and yellow in the sunlight, could be seen diving and surfacing on their underwater quests at infrequent intervals.

Now, back at the camp, Major Moore explained: 'The decontamination work on land is still going on but even that may be ended soon because it seems more likely the device landed in the sea.

'Right now we're going up to Site Three where one of the bombs fell.'

We boarded a bus and minutes later drove out of the camp, past the mine ruins, past the hills near where the burying pit was located, past the bumpy road leading to the cemetery, and along the track on the outskirts of the village by the church. Half-a-mile further on was the white-washed square building, housing one of the village's electric transformers, and here the bus turned sharp right off the track which had been heavily sprayed with water to avoid the spread of dust.

'This, gentlemen, is Site Three,' announced the major. 'Come on out and have a look round.'

It was the same spot where nearly a month before I had witnessed the strange scene of the masked men in white digging up contaminated soil near the screened-off area around the bomb crater.

How things had changed! The gaping crater, blasted in the soil by the bomb's TNT detonator charge, had been completely filled in. A water main ruptured by the non-nuclear explosion had been repaired. A wall which had been flattened was being rebuilt. And the orange flag marking the bomb's location had been taken down. In fact, the Americans were restoring the site so well it would soon be impossible to tell that a bomb had dropped there at all.

The two farmhouses near the spot were still deserted. Around one of the buildings, two scientists from the Spanish Nuclear Commission were making radioactivity tests by holding alpha scintillation meters close to the walls. Readings on the counters were being jotted down on charts. A blue American Air Force staff car drove up and parked behind our bus. Out strode a fatigue-clad officer. It was Colonel White, the man in charge of the decontamination work. A blue mask was slung under his chin, and he talked openly about what had happened when the bombs plunged around Palomares.

'The force of impact of the weapon which landed here caused its TNT charge to detonate. A large crater was blasted in the ground and the nuclear materials in the core were sprayed out,' he explained, confirming exactly what Sergeant Haley had described almost a month before.

'Unfortunately, there was a strong breeze at the time and

this carried the nuclear particles over a large area of fields for nearly a mile.'

The Colonel walked over to the bluff of the hillside overlooking the sea and pointed down towards the fields below where the red and white flags had been replaced by green ones.

'We had to strip all those fields as a precaution. The topsoil has been removed and the earth hosed and ploughed. There is no danger of contamination now, and the villagers will be able to plant new crops.

'Of course, at the time we had to take certain precautions, so two or three farmhouses in this immediate area were evacuated. However, the occupants will soon be able to return to their homes. It is perfectly safe now.'

I asked the colonel if it was true that the H-bombs around Palomares had fallen practically in a line. 'That's right,' he replied. 'They landed about a mile apart.'

Was this because the B-52 crew had been unable to jettison these three bombs properly, unlike the missing fourth weapon believed to be attached to its parachute? 'Maybe that's what happened.'

What about the bomb which landed by the Moorish fort? 'It was partly buried in the ground, but fell intact. There was no danger of radioactivity there although the earth around the weapon was removed as a further precaution.'

The third bomb? 'That landed beyond the village near the cemetery in the hills. The detonating charge of that one also exploded and we are still decontaminating the area. You cannot go there today.'

How long did it take to find the three bombs? 'They were all located within 18 hours of the crash.'

Any clues where the lost H-bomb might be? 'None. But my guess is that it's in the sea.'

Colonel White refused to answer only one question.

How is the contaminated soil being sent to America? 'No comment!'

I was soon to discover the answer. Thousands of coffins were at that moment being prepared for the most bizarre funeral procession ever to cross the Atlantic.

The sun shone – coldly. The breeze stiffened – freshly. And

the U.S. ambassador donned his blue swimming trunks – somewhat reluctantly. The day of Mr Duke's much-publicised 'Big Dip' had barely dawned. The moment of icy truth was at hand. And a moment of light relief!

After all, the ambassador had been the one who had suggested the swim at Palomares in the first place. It was his idea to give visual proof to potential holidaymakers that there was positively no danger of anyone stubbing their toe on the missing warhead or becoming contaminated. There was no backing out now.

As Mr Duke changed, and shivered at the very thought of taking the plunge, a battery of TV cameras was being set up on the beach and scores of newsmen and photographers jostled for positions on the sand.

The Mediterranean, a sparkling blue, waited – very calm and very cold.

There have been many strange things in the past which diplomats have had to suffer in the line of duty. This was surely the strangest of them all: an envoy volunteering to swim near a submerged H-bomb before breakfast?

So, shortly after 9.30 that nippy Tuesday morning the ambassador, wearing a blue bathing cap and bathrobe, trotted bravely and barefoot down to the beach.

'How's the water?' he asked, forcing a smile to hide his already-chattering teeth.

'Freezing!' was the unanimous and hardly encouraging reply. The ambassador grimaced. 'Anyone care to join me?'

No one among the assembled ranks of the world's Press moved. The slimly-built diplomat suppressed a shiver as he slowly slipped off his bathrobe. In the background a Spanish waiter, smartly attired in tails and bow-tie, stood by ready to administer first aid. Resting on his arm was a silver tray with a solitary glass and a bottle of bracing cognac.

It wasn't the thought of an H-bomb lying in the water, possibly emitting radioactivity, that prompted the journalists' non-participation. Not even the fear of getting contaminated. It was a much more down-to-earth reason. No one wanted to risk catching a cold!

Mr Duke, however, did not face a lone ordeal. He had wisely taken the precaution of mustering moral support by inviting some of his embassy colleagues to leave the cosy comfort of their heated offices to join the swim-in Diplomatically, how could they refuse.

So here they all were, lining up on the sand, clasping woolly towels to hide their goose-pimples, and rubbing their hands to keep their circulations going.

There was Mr William W. Walker, Minister at the embassy, Mr Mel Niswander, the Press Attaché, Mr Bell, the Information Officer, and Mr Tim Towel, the ambassador's aide. Even General Donovan turned out in regulation trunks to represent the armed forces.

'Go on then, in you go!' shouted an impatient villager.

The intrepid ambassador scampered hastily across the sand and into the sea, splashing extra loudly to hide the gasping shock of the cold. Close behind followed the gallant diplomatic corps in their do-or-die display of loyalty, along with Mr Duke's two children Marilu, aged 11, and Dario, aged 8, plus the son and daughter of Spanish minister Senor Iribarne, Maribel aged 16, and Jose Manuel aged 15, and General Donovan's 11-year-old son, Eric.

'Come on in! It's great!' he invited – unconvincingly. 'Help me find the bomb.'

The cameras whirred and some photographers, in trying to get close-up pictures, were soaked by the waves. Television reporter Harry Debelius, of the American Broadcasting Company, stripped down to his swim suit and, grabbing a microphone and yards of cable, prepared to paddle out for an interview. He stopped short at ankle depth and yelled: 'Sorry, sir, I can't reach you with the mike.'

It was five minutes of farce. Nobody, least of all the ambassador, really expected he might suddenly be stricken by lethal alpha rays in the sea.

But from a propaganda viewpoint it was a great stunt. Already hundreds of pictures had been taken. Thousands of words would be written, and newsfilm of the dip would soon be screened throughout the Western world to accomplish what hours of speeches and volumes of scientific reports would never achieve.

Mr Duke had made his point – the hard way, and the swim-in would have served its purpose of righting some of the many wrongs circulating about Palomares.

Shivering, the ambassador finally emerged from the Mediterranean – to be sent back in again immediately for the exclusive benefit of the CBS television cameras, and then again for the NBC unit. Four times he was sent scurrying back.

His face was blue with cold when he stumbled on to the beach after the final plunge. His hands shook so much he was incapable of lifting a glass of cognac without spilling the lot. This was probably why he declined a warming nip.

Despite the cold a dripping Mr Duke patiently repeated well-rehearsed replies to the ensuing barrage of questions.

How was the swim? 'It was exhilarating and sensational. It reminded me very much of Jones' beach on a memorial day week-end.'

Do you think that you have proved there is no danger by swimming in the sea?

'I think that this area, which is probably one of the most magnificent tourist areas of all Europe with the finest climate of this part of the world, has so much to offer that I think we have, in effect, given emphasis to the scientists' – both American and Spanish – contentions from the very beginning that there is no danger to public health in this coastal region, and not a trace whatsoever of radioactivity in the water.'

Did you by any chance stub your toe on the bomb while you were out there? 'Wish I had!'

The ordeal of the swim – so the ambassador mistakenly thought – was at last over.

An hour later, after breakfast and a hot bath, he drove to 'Campamento Wilson' to greet Senor Iribarne and a party of Spanish government officials, including the Air Minister, General Lacalle Larraga, who were scheduled to arrive by helicopter at Palomares from San Javier.

General Wilson eventually gave the envoy and the two ministers a detailed briefing in his tent headquarters and then they drove into Palomares where over 1,000 turned out to greet them, cheering and waving banners which read: 'The American troops have done right by us.' 'Palomares and its beaches need roads – help us.' 'Please make Palomares a holiday centre.'

They later spoke to the authorities at Cuevas de Almanzora and Villaricos and listened to the problems presented by several villagers before returning to the camp.

It was at this point that Senor Iribarne reminded the ambassador of the swim they had planned together. 'But I've already been in once . . .' he began to protest.

But, again, there was no diplomatic escape. Mr Duke borrowed a pair of trunks from a U.S. Navy SCUBA diver and joined the minister and several Spanish officials for his second swim within three hours.

Senor Iribarne's trip from Madrid that Tuesday was primarily for the inauguration of a new luxury government hotel, Los Reyes Catolicos, the fiftieth Parador to be opened in Spain and located in the foothills of the Sierra Cabrera range.

It was during a series of speeches at the opening ceremony that afternoon that Mr Duke recalled the day of the crash and said: 'For the people of Almeria it was as if the hand of God reached out to spare them from harm. Not one living thing was injured in any way, either by the falling wreckage or the nuclear material which the aircraft was carrying.'

He said the tragedy 'has brought us face to face with a set of realities which has turned the eyes of the world upon this coast and its community of Palomares.'

Mr Duke said the decontamination process was still going on. 'It will continue until Spanish and American scientists are satisfied that we are leaving Spain as we found it. Areas already cleaned are now ready for planting again of the next crops. There is not the slightest risk in eating products of the area – tomatoes, fruit, fish or milk. The waters along the coast are being tested continuously for radioactivity at many depths but not a trace has been found.

'Life is returning to normal here after what has surely been a crisis. There has been no hysteria, no panic. The people of Palomares are, like the people of the rest of the world, interested and concerned, involved and questioning but determined to face the realities of the changing world. None of us can discern our future in the atomic age we live, but we do know it is an age with which we must come to terms.'

Spain's tourist figures were already up 13 per cent during the first two months of the year, compared to 1965. And one holidaymaker, at least, had come to terms with the lost H-bomb. Along the coast, not far from Palomares, the first bikini girl of the 1966 season stretched out on the sand, seeking a sun-tan.

CHAPTER NINE

A N INCREDIBLE number of mysterious objects were being located on the seabed by the divers, scanning sonar, acoustical devices and underwater craft. By Wednesday, March 9, exactly 358 contacts had been made by Task Force 65. Over 100 of these still had to be investigated. Obviously, a considerable portion of the blazing B-52 had scattered in the Mediterranean during its death plunge – much more than was originally estimated.

The Alvin, Aluminaut and Cubmarine were being worked to their limits – diving, exploring, attaching lift lines, surfacing to re-charge batteries and diving again. Any one of those contacts already made could be the lost bomb.

In the operations room aboard the cruiser Boston was a scale model of the ocean floor, giving the appearance of a craggy mountain range. Coloured pins had been inserted at the various spots where wreckage had either been found or objects had been buoyed for recovery.

Admiral Guest realised that most of the objects would be ordinary wreckage. But from underwater photographs of 14 of the contacts he knew that there was also some top-secret equipment to be winched to the surface.

'Our efforts were directed towards recovering all debris and classified material not yet located and picked up ashore,' he recalled. 'This included classified material which might have helped to analyse the cause of the crash.

'Our forces included about 120 of the Navy's best frogmen and deep sea divers. We had the latest equipment available, some proven in naval operations, some experimental and fresh off the drawing boards, and some provided by civilian contractors who were specialists in underwater operations.

'Although the sea was our medium, we faced many difficulties. The task was anything but simple.

'No one could state with certainty the exact geographical

point at which the aircraft collided – nor was it possible to calculate the exact trajectory of the parts of the disintegrated aircraft. Our oceanographic analysts had reviewed reports from the Air Force which, coupled with debris recovered, established a pattern indicating the areas of "highest probability" as to where the bomb might be.'

The Admiral emphasised the problems which faced the recovery operation by indicating a scale model. 'The underwater terrain in this area was extremely rugged. There were canyons and ravines with depths over 3,600 feet. There were subterranean hills. And the bottom, in some sections, was dotted with rocks and coral heads.

'These factors greatly complicated the use of electronic and acoustic search equipment – like underwater television and sonar – and in many sections we resorted to purely visual searches in deep water, where visibility was only about ten feet. This required patience and painstaking and time-consuming effort.'

Commencing with the arrival of Task Force 65, tests for radiation and contamination of sea water by collecting numerous samples at various depths each day, had been started. None of these samples indicated the presence of radiation. In addition, coring samples were taken of the mud on the bottom in widespread locations. The results were all negative. Admiral Guest revealed that when about 175 pieces of aircraft wreckage and classified equipment had been recovered, it was found that some were major sections of aircraft wing, while others weighed as little as a few ounces and were only a few square inches in size. This, he said, gave an approximation of the thoroughness of the sea search.

While the search was still going on, the Admiral said, to the dismay of the Spanish Authorities: 'I do not expect this to be a short, quick operation. We may be here for a considerable period before we have accomplished our mission.' There was every indication that the sea search – in which more scientific knowledge of underwater exploration was being gleaned every day – might drag on for another six months, or a year, or more.

'The bomb must be recovered at all costs', had been the stern directive of the military chiefs at the Pentagon, spurred on by the Defence Department, and confirmed by President Johnson himself. There was to be no respite until the coded signal

'Instrument Panel' had been sent by the pilot of one of the submersibles to the surface, and until the H-bomb had been hauled aboard one of the warships.

On land, the hunt was petering out in disappointing failure. Only 200 troops remained to scour the barren countryside for the nuclear weapon.

General Wilson said the main task of finding all the wreckage around Palomares and disposing of it had been completed. Altogether 265.7 acres of farmland had been made 'almost surgically clean' by ploughing and removing the topsoil. All the quarantined fields had now been handed back to the villagers in the area. Melon growers, in fact, were already planting seeds and, following American advice, were adopting for the first time twentieth century methods of speeding the growth of their crops by using thin, Polythene sheets to cover their fields.

Two days later, back in Madrid – and none the worse for his swim – Senor Iribarne, reporting to General Franco at a cabinet meeting in the Cortes, announced that the 'Broken Arrow' operation on land would end on March 20, but that the search at sea would continue.

'Only a small claims office will be maintained on land,' he added.

Meanwhile, unconfirmed reports came from Palomares of an important find on the seabed: the tailplates of the missing bomb. They were discovered by the Aluminaut on one of its routine dives to investigate a contact. There was no sign of the actual H-bomb, but the find practically convinced Admiral Guest, General Wilson and all the other U.S. officials that the bomb was definitely in the sea.

The tailplates, spotted on the underwater television of the submersible, had been hauled to the surface after lift lines were attached. It seemed likely that they had broken off the warhead on impact with the water and that the bomb, its parachute billowing out underwater, had been carried further out to sea by strong tidal currents.

*　　*　　*

The secret of how the contaminated soil of Palomares was to be spirited away to America was, at last, revealed in a sinister, macabre scene as hundreds of sealed blue barrels were laid out neatly in rows on the deserted holiday beach. These were the same mysterious barrels seen a month previously, lying outside one of the tent-headquarters, where the huge wooden crates for transporting the soil had been made. Then they were empty. Now they were full.

Altogether there were over 1,200 barrels – actually 55-gallon oil drums – lined up on the sand. Each one contained 500 lbs of radioactive dirt, together with contaminated tomato vines and other vegetation. Each one was welded shut and additionally sealed with steel bars. Eventually there would be nearly 5,000 barrels.

The poisoned earth was awaiting shipment to the 80-acre burial plot for atomic waste in the United States. Soon the barrels – or 'coffins' as some of the troops had nicknamed them – would be loaded on to a cargo ship, U.S.N.S. Boyce, for the weirdest of trans-Atlantic crossings to Charleston, South Carolina.

The beach was a hive of activity as preparations for the Nuclear Age 'funeral procession' reached a climax. Landing craft No. 1492 was beached and its flat bows lowered on to the sand, ready for the first barrels to be rolled aboard. A bulldozer was flattening out a vast area of the beach for more barrels to be stacked. In the background were the few remaining tents of 'Campamento Wilson' and a caterpillar crane was being used to help lift off some of the barrels from blue-painted military lorries. Fork lift trucks churned through the sand, and regular convoys of lorries were being maintained along a heavily-watered track from the beach, up into the hills behind Palomares.

Hidden in the cluster of hills, still patrolled by armed Spanish Guardia Civiles, the strange task of filling up hundreds more barrels continued in secret.

This was at the nuclear burial site, where 6,000 tons of in-fected earth had already been taken in wooden crates from the fields during the two hectic months of the 'Broken Arrow' operation.

Men in surgical masks, skull caps, white protective clothing and rubber boots taped to stop even the tiniest speck of dust from entering, were engaged in a 'mass exhumation.'

Soil buried in large pits some weeks before was being dug

up and shovelled into heaps. Scientists tested for alpha rays with electronic counters, sifting among the stale-smelling brown earth, shrivelled vines and rotten vegetation. Then, if traces of radioactivity, however mild, were still found the earth was dumped into the barrels and at the same time hosed down.

The lids of the barrels clanged shut and were sealed to ensure that no invisible particles of H-bomb dust could leak out during the 3,000-mile voyage.

The barrels were loaded on to the waiting lorries for the bumpy, downhill journey to the beach, where each one was being carefully numbered. Floodlights had been set up around the precious 'coffins' and Air Force police patrolled the beach day and night.

A little chunk of Spain, mingling with the fragments of two hydrogen bombs, would soon be on the first leg of its journey to a permanent burial place in America.

The U.S. decision to ship the earth to the Atomic Energy Commission's Savannah River plant, near Aiken, South Carolina, was to crush for ever fears among Spaniards that harm could come to them or their visitors by the presence of a nuclear burial ground, less than a mile from what would eventually become a booming holiday beach.

Upon arrival at the naval port of Charleston the Spanish soil would be scientifically examined by A.E.C. inspectors and federal agricultural experts. Its final resting place would be in trenches 350 feet long, 20 feet deep and 20 feet wide. I would be bulldozed under 10 feet of virgin dirt.

Residents of the Aiken area, aware that radioactive wastes had been buried at the Savannah River plant since 1952, expressed no fear over the plan to dispose of approximately 1,100 tons of mildly contaminated dirt and tomato vines from Spain in the atomic graveyard.

Curiously, this site had seen its first Spanish visitor over four centuries before, when the explorer Hernando de Soto, arrived there searching for Indian gold and silver.

*　　　*　　　*

Fifty-seven days after the B-52 disaster, prospects of recovering the H-bomb could not have appeared more bleak. On land, the 'Broken Arrow' operation was being phased down. A vast, desert-like area extending in a semi-circle around Palomares, from the north eastern port of Aguilas, inland, to Huercal Overa and south west along the coast beyond Carboneras, had been systematically searched by troops, spotter planes and helicopters. Not a flicker of radioactivity on the alpha scintillation meters had indicated where the bomb might be.

At sea, results had been equally disappointing. Ships continued to scour within the triangular zone of 'high probability' but it had become more of a salvage operation than a hunt. The frogmen, hard-hat and SCUBA divers had retrieved most of the seabed objects located at depths in which they were safely able to work. Now, it was up to the submersibles to continue the quest in deeper waters.

Certain modifications had been urgently required for the Alvin's grappling claw and the necessary equipment had been flown out to Spain from San Diego, after a delay. This, it was felt, would enable the sub to operate more effectively by attaching lift lines with its claw to debris or the bomb.

Another major handicap for the pilots and observers in the underwater craft was poor visibility below 1,000 feet. It had been necessary to install auxiliary lights on both the Alvin and Aluminaut.

Lieutenant-Commander Brad Mooney, Admiral Guest's adviser on the use and capabilities of the deep submergence vehicles, explained a further setback. 'We were handicapped by the inability to use any type of magnetic search equipment. The area was a veritable lead and zinc mine, and, from the air, veins of metal showed clearly.

'The sonar search was exceptionally accurate on recording configuration. A combination of three types of scanner had found hundreds of contacts. Most of them, however, proved to be terrain.'

Frequent bouts of bad weather also brought the sea hunt to a temporary halt on a number of occasions. Added the commander: 'The people of Palomares told us it never rained, or hadn't in eight years. But it rained almost every day we were here. They blamed it all on the bomb!'

* * *

Senor Simo, the fisherman, duly directed the U.S. Navy – for the third time – to the spot where he had first seen the parachutes splash down. Again he relied on his uncanny skill to get there; again it was within a few hundred yards of where he had previously indicated, and again it was outside the zone of 'high probability' pin-pointed by the scientific experts.

To double check his position, the fisherman, standing on the deck of his boat near the helm, took a set of compass bearings to eastwards, and another set of bearings, to north and north-east, by lining-up on the mountain peaks on land over six miles away. These bearings were pencilled in on a chart and at the points where they crossed Senor Simo stabbed a pin into the chart and said confidently: 'That's the spot where the parachutes fell. And that's the spot where we are right now.'

There were those who doubted the accuracy of his sighting, but finally a second zone of high probability, $5\frac{1}{2}$ to 6 miles off the Palomares coast, and in an area of 27.33 square miles, was established from his eyewitness accounts and the three trips to the same spot.

One of the U.S. Navy experts who firmly believed Senor Simo was Commander Mooney. 'We had been operating in a pattern from the shore out,' he recalled. 'This fisherman said the bomb went into the water at a spot farther out.

'I had a hunch he was right. When the overdue equipment for the Alvin finally arrived the technicians asked for two days to test it.

'I suggested immediate tests in the deep water, near the spot the fisherman had pointed out. Otherwise, it would be weeks before the submersibles extended their search to that area.'

So, shortly after dawn on Tuesday, March 15, the Alvin, its batteries fully charged and with its new claw clamped on, rested on the floodable deck of the landing ship dock Fort Snelling, waiting to be launched. The two pilots, Valentine Wilson and Marvin McCamis, climbed up the three steps on the side of the conning tower and lowered themselves into the tiny craft. Half-an-hour later, seawater gushed into the well-deck and the tiny sub was towed out into the Gulf of Vera towards the new established zone of Senor Simo's sightings.

Shadowed by the submarine rescue ship Petrel, it nosed through the heaving swell and prepared to dive not far from where the minesweeper Rival was circling.

The sky was cloudy, but at 9.20 a.m., when the Alvin slowly disappeared in a hiss of bubbling foam, the sun cut through the water to cast an eerie silver reflection on the hull of the craft as it flitted down into the deep.

The pencil beams of the Alvin's lights pierced the underwater gloom. Visibility became murkier and murkier. The needle of the fathometer moved up to 50 fathoms, then 100, 150 and 200.

There was a clammy heat inside the cockpit. Sweat beaded on Wilson's forehead as he concentrated on the mass of instruments on the panel in front of him. The scanning sonar bleeped out its messages, and the screen of the closed circuit television alternated from a fuzzy grey to a white haze as the lights illuminated the shadowy depths.

At 2,500 feet, the seabed had almost been reached. Wilson steered carefully, knowing the dangers of perhaps burying the snout of the Alvin into an underwater mountainside of mud, and becoming trapped.

The dangers were, indeed, immense. With visibility cut to a mere ten feet the two pilots could barely discern the outline of the surrounding canyons, gullies and crevices.

The descent had taken over an hour. Now, the Alvin set out to explore the ocean floor. It gingerly inched its way along the valleys and up the steeply-rising slopes, its rear propeller sending up clouds of swirling mud and sand as the sub, at times, almost scraped the bottom.

For ninety minutes, the pilots listened vainly for the tell-tale warning on the scanning sonar of an underwater object. Their eyes were red-rimmed through staring at the television screen, which aided the delicate manoeuvres of the vessel, and through the large observation window in the conning tower.

Seaweed curled up menacingly, like the grasping tentacles of an octopus trying to ensnare its prey. The seabed was rocky in some places, muddy in others. Needle-sharp coral heads protruded from the slime, and the occasional inquisitive fish cautiously circled the man-made monster of the deep.

There was no sound or sign of any contact being made. The only noise was the muffled throb of the Alvin's motor as it propelled itself both horizontally and vertically through the water.

Then, at 11.50 a.m. the sub steered up a 70-degree slope. Visibility was reduced to eight feet, at a depth of 2,550 feet. The pilots were preparing to abandon their probe, surface and dive elsewhere.

Suddenly, the sonar bleeped urgently. The Alvin closed in on the object it had detected, about a mile from the position indicated by Senor Simo.

Both Wilson and McCamis were gripped by excitement. They did not speak a word. They kept their eyes glued outside into the subterranean gloom.

The Alvin hovered above a 20-foot-wide gully, on the slope, its powerful lights beaming into the darkness. The ooze of the seabed, looking rather like freshly poured cement, was at least six to ten feet deep. The two civilian explorers peered towards the gully, but a slight movement on one side distracted their gaze.

'Look! Down there!' instructed Wilson tensely. 'Do you see it? There's definitely something embedded in the mud!'

A few seconds later, a voice from the deep, hoarse and excited, crackled through the sonar telephone in the minesweeper Rival. 'Instrument panel! Instrument panel!'

*   *   *

Admiral Guest prayed that the signal was not a false alarm, consulted his Chief of Staff, Captain Page, and gave instructions for a briefing of senior officers to be called immediately aboard the Boston, where the 'ops' room was a scene of suppressed excitement and cool efficiency.

Assistance would have to be sent down to the Alvin – rapidly. There was only one other craft capable of taking part in a recovery bid at such a pressure-crushing depth: the Aluminaut.

But the sister sub was currently out of action and in dry dock having its batteries re-charged. Commander Mooney, after consultations with Jon Lindbergh, sent an urgent message across to the captain of the Privateer, Master C. Morris. Aboard this support and tracking ship the Aluminaut's pilots, Robert Serfass and Robert Canary, were told to stand by to take their craft down for a rendezvous with the Alvin, the moment its batteries were fully charged.

Down below, on the seabed, Wilson and McCamis – on the instructions of their surface controller, Mr Rainnie, – had daringly edged the Alvin in for close-up photographs of the object they had spotted. The full glare of the sub's spotlights tried to pick out the object and the lens of the television camera was trained towards the gully.

It was a delicate operation, fraught with dangers. If the submersible went in too close its propellers would disturb the ooze, sending up a blanket of clouding mud. The Alvin might then collide with the object and perhaps knock it off the edge of the gully into a narrow crevice of unknown depth, into which the sub would not be able to follow. Also, there was the fear that if the object was the missing bomb a sudden jolt might detonate the conventional TNT charge, with disastrous results.

The object certainly resembled descriptions of the bomb given to the pilots. Despite being practically buried in the ooze, it could be seen that it was cylindrical and, more important, was half hidden by the folds of a billowing parachute. It appeared to be intact.

For nearly four hours, the pint-sized Alvin poised above the object, taking a number of photographs for later enlargement and examination.

Wilson and McCamis were ordered to stay put on the seabed, to switch out their lights, cut the motor and conserve their batteries as much as possible. Already the Alvin had been submerged for over six hours. Normally it surfaced after eight hours to re-charge its batteries and to undergo other vital maintenance checks.

The pilots turned the bulbous craft sideways and gently plopped it down into the gully alongside the object. And there the Alvin stayed, like a lioness guarding a cub, occasionally rolling in the ooze from the force of the tidal currents.

From their precarious position, Wilson and McCamis maintained sonar telephone contact with the surface ships of Task Force 65, while awaiting the arrival of the Aluminaut. For the two men it was a nerve-racking ordeal, sweating in the cramped darkness of their craft. It was not until later that afternoon that the sister sub was despatched to the scene. But at last, the most complicated salvage operation of all times was underway.

Never before had recovery of an object as heavy as a H-bomb

been successful at such a colossal depth.

The Aluminaut took down with it a sonar transponder – an electronic gadget for attachment to the object or its parachute, so that the object could be relocated for subsequent lifting operations if it became lost again. The transponder would be able to receive an underwater radar signal from a searching sub and reflect it back on a different frequency, so as to avoid any interference on the same wavelength.

It took the Aluminaut over an hour to dive to 2,550 feet and locate the parked Alvin, even with its continuous transmission FM scanning sonar.

The rendezvous was a wonderful achievement for the Americans. It was the first rendezvous of two manned submersibles in deep inner space. But it was only just in time. The Alvin could not have stayed on guard much longer over the bomb.

The Aluminaut stood by as the Alvin slowly rose up from the mud, illuminating the manoeuvre with its auxiliary lights. Once clear of the gully, the little craft commenced a slow ascent to the surface so that the film could be developed and examined and the pilots closely questioned.

For the relief sub it was the beginning of a 24-hour endurance watch. No effort would be made to lift the object until it could be identified positively by the photographs, and braided nylon lines could be attached for the big haul to the surface.

Certainly, the claws of both the Alvin and the Aluminaut would not be strong enough to raise anything as large as a nuclear bomb from the ocean floor. Something else would have to be done.

So, initially, the Aluminaut set about the task of attaching the transponder to the parachute to enable the submersibles to 'home' on the bomb again. This was successfully achieved after nearly three hours of patient manipulation of the robot grappling arm.

The pilots, Serfass and Canary, reported this success to the Privateer on the surface above and Admiral Guest, who was already studying rushed enlargements of the underwater pictures taken by the Alvin, was notified.

The pictures, although a little blurred, grainy and grey because of the poor visibility on the seabed, clearly showed a metallic object buried in the mud and partly obscured by a tangled parachute. The Admiral breathed a long sigh of relief as he and his advisers looked at the photographs and confirmed that they were of the missing H-bomb.

Senor Simo, the fisherman, using his rough and ready navigational methods, had been right all the time.

The Spaniard had confounded the efforts of all the U.S. Navy experts, with their scientific calculations, to locate the spot by establishing zones from the pattern of debris and patterns established by divers, sophisticated sonar and acoustical devices.

*   *   *

As in the case of the actual crash of the B-52, news of the apparent discovery of the lost H-bomb was flashed from Europe to the United States. Admiral Guest first radioed details ashore to General Wilson and Spanish Air Force General Montel Pouzet, at the Palomares beach headquarters.

All communications were in code as a standard precaution against spies and foreign powers line-tapping and learning of the dramatic development. Although the Russian trawler had disappeared beyond the horizon it was still lurking somewhere within 20 miles of the search zone, and was obviously monitoring all signals.

The find was referred to as 'Contact 261', and Admiral Guest selected the name of his eldest son Robert as the code word for the object, and the name of his son Douglas as code word for the parachute.

General Halloway, Commander-in-Chief of the U.S. Air Force in Europe, was one of the first to receive the top-secret communiqué from Spain at his headquarters in Wiesbaden, Germany. In Washington, President Johnson was immediately informed. The sustained flap in the Pentagon, provoked to almost hysterical proportions by the persistent Russian attacks, calmed down, and Defence Department chiefs were delighted with the encouraging news.

In Madrid, General Franco was officially notified along with the Air Minister, General Lacalle Larraga. Mr Duke, the ambassador, was briefed by General Donovan at Torrejon airbase.

Two days were to elapse, however, before the world was to find out that America had tracked down and was fishing for its missing H-bomb.

The news was to provide a world news 'scoop' for Harry Stathos, then chief of the Madrid bureau of UPI.

But it was a story he was to stumble across in the oddest circumstances – 20,000 feet up in a German airliner jetting between Frankfurt and the Spanish capital.

Reports of the find on the seabed had circulated among senior officers at the base in Wiesbaden. Two topics dominated their leisure conversation, apart from wives, girl friends or frauleins – the developments in the Vietnamese war and the bomb hunt in Spain.

During an off-duty drink, a U.S. colonel casually remarked to a German friend, who was a pilot for the Lufthansa airline, that he understood the bomb had probably been located offshore from Palomares. He gave details of how the Alvin had nosed down towards the object and its parachute on the seabed, and how it was hoped to attach lift lines and winch up the bomb within three or four days.

Twelve hours later, early on Thursday morning, March 17, the pilot boarded a plane at Frankfurt for a few days holiday in Madrid. Also on the aircraft, returning to his office, was Stathos, who had been in Frankfurt making final arrangements following a recent promotion to take over the German news desk.

Stathos had covered the bomb story in Spain from the very beginning. Shortly after take-off he began talking to the young pilot occupying the seat alongside him in the tourist compartment. Eventually the conversation switched to Palomares.

'I expect you know all about the bomb being found?' queried the pilot in a thick guttural accent. 'My American Air Force colonel friend told me last night it should be lifted out of the sea by the week-end.'

Stathos was taken aback by the pilot's revelations. There had been no official announcement or hint about the bomb being located. But there was little he could do about checking out the facts in the jet high above the sprawling French countryside.

Two hours later, however, back in his Madrid office after a dash from the airport, he made two phone calls.

The first was to the American embassy and the second to

Torrejon airbase. Both times he asked the same question: 'Is it true the bomb has been found?' On both occasions the firm answer was 'No comment!'

And, judging from earlier experiences on the bomb story, 'No comment!' meant that there was something afoot and that the Americans had clamped down the veil of secrecy again.

Stathos pursued his inquiries and less than an hour later his bulletin scoop, under a Frankfurt dateline, was tapped out on the world's wires: 'U.S. officials are almost certain that the missing H-bomb has been located in the Mediterranean off the coast of Palomares, Spain, and recovery operations have started...'

Two hours afterwards Mr Bell, the Information Officer at the embassy, cautiously confirmed: 'There have been hopeful developments but I cannot give any further information at this time. If we have positive identification and recovery a statement will be made.'

The identity of the man who had led the Americans to their H-bomb was soon discovered. Francisco Simo was about to become a national hero.

The fisherman of Aguilas had just returned home from the sea and was having supper with his dark-haired wife, Rosita, and his two young children, Alfonso and Rosa Maria, when the phone rang. He was unaware of the Americans' find but news was spreading like wildfire around the tiny port that an object attached to a parachute had been located at the spot Senor Simo had pointed out.

'They've found it! I knew I was right!' he yelled excitedly, after replacing the phone receiver. The Spaniard hugged his astonished wife. 'The bomb! It's down there in the sea just where I said it would be!'

That same evening in Madrid, a midnight news briefing was called by ambassador Mr Duke – then abruptly cancelled. No explanation was given but top-level decisions were being made in Washington, and one of them by the Secretary of State, Mr Rusk, was warning that the trumpets of triumph should not be blown until after the bomb had been safely recovered.

As it turned out, this was a wise move. Unforeseen complications were about to baulk efforts to retrieve the stubborn H-bomb from the seabed.

CHAPTER TEN

JUST OVER five miles offshore from Palomares and Garrucha, U.S Navy ships loomed above the spot where, 2,550 feet below, the drama of the deep was being enacted. But it was more than a question of dive, grab and surface, as the crews of the Alvin and Aluminaut were finding out.

The submersibles were taking it in turns, working to the limits of their endurance, to dive down and try to hook life lines to the shrouds of the parachute. On the seabed there was no distinction between night and day – just perpetual darkness – and the object, frequently located by pencil beams of light, defied all the first recovery attempts. It seemed to bury itself deeper in the ooze, and in doing so inched nearer and nearer to the edge of the gully.

Admiral Guest ordered extreme caution to be exercised in any recovery bid, for by Saturday, March 19, it had become obvious that the hoped-for quick 'grab' was not going to be realised. It was decided, therefore, to attempt to hook an anchor into the parachute so that it could be dragged with the bomb along the seabed, to a safer position for hauling it to the surface.

While not yet admitting that it was the bomb which had been found, an official statement from Task Force 65 said: 'With regard to the unidentified object and attached parachute at a depth of some 2,500 feet about five miles off the shores from Palomares, Admiral Guest has advised that because of the extremely steep slope of the sea bottom on which the object and parachute are resting, it is proposed to attempt first to move them to a more favourable recovery area. If successful, this course of action will lessen the risk of having the object fall from its present precarious position into much deeper water. When the object is positively identified, an appropriate announcement will be made.'

Mr Bell, at the U.S. embassy in Madrid, stressed that the danger of the bomb's conventional TNT detonator exploding, rupturing the casing and spreading plutonium and uranium in the Mediterranean during the delicate dragging operation, was 'slight.' There was no possibility of a nuclear blast, as the bomb was unarmed. And the only formality – apart from the actual recovery – was to check the bomb's serial number, just to make sure it was the right one, and that there were no other stray H-bombs rolling around on the seabed!

But that afternoon, sudden squalls returned to Palomares. Winds increased to 35 knots and the seas mounted to such an extent that submersible operations had to be cancelled.

The Aluminaut had, in any case, developed electrical trouble and had been towed to the port of Garrucha, accompanied by the tracking vessel Privateer, for the batteries to be re-charged and for minor repairs.

The intervention of the weather was yet another crisis threatening the success of the entire operation. Admiral Guest's plan, after dragging the object to a safer position, had been for the Alvin or Aluminaut to attach a three-inch thick nylon line, enabling the bomb to be winched up on the 20-ton capacity boom of the salvage ship Hoist.

Now, the rough seas were likely to be disturbing the seabed and there was a risk of treacherous underwater tidal currents dislodging the bomb. There was absolutely nothing to be done other than wait until the bad weather abated.

Tension was etched on the faces of all those engaged on the search as the strain of enforced inactivity began to show. Admiral Guest paced the operations room aboard the Boston, deep in thought and inwardly cursing the elements. Captain Page, his Chief of Staff, called hopefully for another long-range weather forecast. Commanders Springer and Mooney held earnest conversations, discussing prospects of recovery if the underwater currents had dislodged the bomb from its precarious perch. The rested and restless crews of the Alvin and Aluminaut stood by, eagerly awaiting the command that would send the subs diving back down to their target in the ooze.

Fate seemed determined to thwart the Americans in all their attempts to raise the sunken H-bomb.

The main fear was that by now the bomb might have tumbled off the gully, into the crevice. If this was the case, drastic tactics would have to be adopted to get to grips with the weapon again.

The crevice, approximately five feet wide and of unknown depth, could comfortably swallow the bomb but its mouth was far too small for the Alvin to enter. It would have to be blasted open with time-fused explosives, an extremely dangerous operation, as explosives had never been used before for blasting rock at such a great depth. There was also the possibility of the bomb's conventional TNT charge being set off, thus cracking open the casing.

The U.S. Navy specialists just prayed that this course of action would not have to be taken and that the bomb had not moved during the squalls.

They were not to find out until the morning of Wednesday, March 23, when the winds finally dropped and the high seas calmed. The Alvin once more ventured forth from the sheltered dock of the Fort Snelling, and at last, the plan of recovery was again in action.

It took the Alvin over an hour to make the descent, weaving between sheer underwater cliffs over 100 feet high. The two pilots intently scanned their sonar, trying to pick up the reflected radar signal from the transponder which had been attached to the parachute.

Contact 261 soon answered the Alvin's call. Visibility was poor, but with the aid of the searchlights the grubby folds of the parachute were once more spotted, flapping gently in the currents. The object had barely moved from its embedded position on the gully.

Wilson and McCamis relayed a message up to their surface controller and Mr Rainnie informed the relieved Admiral. Underwater blasting would not be necessary after all.

Half an hour later, the salvage ship Hoist steamed back to its position, above where the submersible waited to try and attach a line to drag the bomb along the seabed to a safer position for recovery.

A rescue rig – the three-inch-thick nylon line and anchor with three shorter lines each about 300 feet long attached – was lowered down from the boom.

The Alvin, poised with its grappling arm at the ready to direct the anchor towards the bomb, dared not venture too close, As well as the risk of dislodging the bomb there was the additional problem that even if the line could be secured it might snag on one of the needle-sharp coral rocks – and the nylon would be severed like a knife cutting through butter.

The tiny sub worked to the limits of its endurance but finally, after six frustrating hours, had to acknowledge defeat. Each time it neared the bomb with the anchor the parachute folds settled lazily back into the mud, making it virtually impossible to hook the big catch. The mud was churned up by the propellers of the craft and in the swirling darkness the pilots had to wait anything up to half-an-hour after each attempt before the silt settled and they could spot the object again.

The efforts were so close to success yet equally so close to disaster.

The continued upheaval of the seabed loosened the bomb from its position in the gully and it lurched towards the edge. Fortunately, it moved only two or three feet. But as the Alvin moved in for another bid to hook on the anchor the bomb rolled again, a few more feet nearer to the gaping crevice.

So the little sub was recalled to the surface for its batteries to be recharged and the Aluminaut slipped beneath the waves to take over the trickier-than-ever task.

*   *   *

The whole world looked on expectantly – and, in some cases, critically – as the Americans floundered against the odds to recover their H-bomb. The Soviet government went as far as to propose an international commission to study the incident and witness the recovery, just to make sure the bomb really was hauled up from the seabed and not left there to rust away and contaminate the waters of Spain's south east coast.

As the two subs relentlessly pursued their underwater quest, day and night, it became obvious the chances of fishing the bomb out at all were remote.

It was reported that Jacques Cousteau, the famous undersea explorer, might be called in to give technical assistance to the U.S. Navy. Cousteau, a former French Navy commander and one of the world's most prominent research scientists, had spent hundreds of hours probing the depths of the Mediterranean in his bathysphere. But he was not seen.

In America, Navy chiefs were dismayed by the continued

failure to raise the bomb. In desperation, they assigned another improbable contraption to Admiral Guest's weird underwater fleet. It was a robot vessel called CURV – Cable-Controlled-Underwater-Research-Vehicle.

The CURV looked like a grotesque product of Jules Verne's imagination. It was set on a 15-foot pipebase, similar to the landing gear of a helicopter, and weighed about a ton. Four long red and black ballast tubes for depth control were mounted on the structure together with three electric propulsion motors, mercury vapour lamps, sonar, film and miniature TV cameras, and a detachable claw.

But the robot was still very much in an experimental stage and so far had been used only in the Pacific to help recover 40 spent torpedoes.

There were two snags. Firstly, the maximum depth capability of CURV was only 2,000 feet and the bomb nestled another 550 feet down on the seabed. Scientists at the U.S. Naval Ordnance Test Station, Pasadena, California immediately set to work making major modifications, and the control cable was extended to 2,800 feet, enabling CURV to reach the bomb with 250 feet spare.

Secondly, the claw, resembling a giant nutcracker was only able to clamp itself on objects up to 3 feet wide. The pincers would not be big enough to grasp an H-bomb. The plan was, therefore, to try and manipulate the claw to grab the shrouds of the parachute. CURV would then be backed away, leaving the detachable claw and a buoyed line attached.

The year-old robot had been designed and developed especially for the purpose of continuous deep-submergence search and recovery, and, unlike the Alvin and Aluminaut, would not have to surface periodically for batteries to be re-charged.

Normal operation of CURV required a crew of five: a mechanic, two electronic technicians, a sonar specialist, and a project co-ordinator. After the vehicle had been lowered to the ocean bottom the sonar specialist would direct it towards the target. The electronic technicians would control the vehicle and the claw. And monitoring and manoeuvring would be accomplished from the control console aboard a mother ship.

CURV would 'home' on its target by using high resolution sonar with passive and active modes for co-operative and uncooperative targets, respectively. The target could be photographed with either a 35-mm still camera or the underwater TV unit. Then the hydraulically-operated recovery claw would be positioned and clamped on to the target at the same time as a surface recovery buoy was released.

After CURV backed off, leaving the claw hooked on to the target, the robot would be winched aboard the support ship. Then up would come the catch.

Admiral Guest believed that CURV might be able to succeed where the other craft had so far failed. As he waited for the robot to be flown across the Atlantic another gadget was hooked into the parachute by the Alvin which would emit an acoustic signal to assist CURV in eventually locating the weapon. This was a pinger – a British invention made at the National Institute of Oceanography – which was to play a vital role in the recovery bid.

*   *   *

By Thursday, March 24, the last of exactly 4,810 barrels of contaminated Palomares soil had been loaded aboard the cargo ship Boyce, which that evening set off on the voyage to Charleston, and General Wilson announced: 'I think we have achieved our goal of leaving the Palomares area in the same condition it was in prior to the accident. Considerable support, however, will be required for the continuing operation by the Navy.'

At noon the following day – ten days after Contact 261 had been located – a U.S. Navy communiqué stated: Admiral Guest advises that operations for the recovery of the object with attached parachute are proceeding satisfactorily. These operations must necessarily be accomplished slowly and cautiously, due to the precarious position of the object on a steep slope and the great depths involved. At first, weather conditions with high winds and choppy seas continued periodically to hamper current efforts. The limited endurance of the submersibles being employed and the necessity to recharge their batteries after each dive are primary factors which, with weather, control the tempo of our activity. Everything possible is being done to expedite recovery and identification of the object under these circumstances.'

That Friday afternoon, CURV arrived at the scene after being airlifted from Long Beach, California, international airport. Technicians immediately began the task of re-assembling the robot aboard the submarine rescue ship Petrel.

Admiral Guest had just settled in after transferring his command from the Boston, which had been relieved as flagship of Task Force 65, to a guided missile cruiser, the 18,240-ton U.S.S. Albany (CG-10). Fitted with an extensive array of armament and electronic equipment, including two five-inch guns and menacing clusters of blue and white painted Talos and Tartar missiles, the cruiser took over the role of the Boston by providing logistic and technical support for all ships and units of the Task Force and handling the extensive communications requirements.

The Admiral had rapidly set up his new headquarters in the plotting room aboard the Albany, along with his senior officers, and had briefed the cruiser's commander, Captain J. L. Wohler, on the critical stage reached in the recovery operation.

Later that night, the Alvin dived again to the gully. By now it had made over 100 descents since arriving at Palomares. The crew had gained vital knowledge and experience in operating their bulbous craft at such a depth as 2,550 feet, and patiently stood by as the recovery rig was lowered yet again from the surface. It descended clumsily, yet almost bang on target – the first time the rig had been dropped so near to the bomb.

Wilson and McCamis steered the Alvin towards where the rig rested in the mud. The auxiliary lights blazed eerily as the grappling claw reached out and tugged the line and its anchor across to the half-buried bomb.

First attempts to hook the anchor into the shrouds of the parachute met with familiar failure. They tried, failed and tried again. The early hours of Saturday morning came and soon the Alvin would have to resurface.

Then, as the rig was being dragged through the mud for yet another attempt, the parachute began to billow. The submersible was hovering practically above the bomb. The slimy folds, like the tentacles of an octopus, stretched out, threatening to enmesh and trap the Alvin.

The two pilots spotted the danger through one of the observation windows and hastily steered away from the parachute. But in doing so the anchor was dragged into the folds and hooked tightly on to its elusive quarry. Almost by accident, the hydrogen bomb had been caught.

Excitedly, Wilson and McCamis contacted their surface controller on the sonar telephone, and the captain of the Hoist, Lieutenant-Commander Kane, prepared to lift the warhead off the narrow gully with the boom. The plan was still to try and drag the bomb up the 70 degree slope to a safer recovery position.

The Alvin stood well clear as the actual lift began. The slack nylon line gradually became as taut as a bow string as the boom took the strain.

Would the anchor stay hooked on? Would the billowing silk rip and tear?

Slowly – painfully slowly – the parachute rose up from the ooze. Clouds of mud swirled on the seabed almost blotting out the vision of the pilots.

The silvery grey bomb, as if imprisoned by suction, seemed reluctant to leave its seabed grave. Then, with a final heave, the weapon gurgled inch by inch out of the ooze.

The submerged weight of bomb and parachute was registering between 1,600 and 1,900 pounds. The line, with a breaking strain of over 10,000 pounds, would be able to drag it with ease.

The weapon dangled above the gully. Already, in just over a minute, it had been lifted nearly 30 feet from its precarious perch.

But then, in this moment of triumph, came unexpected disaster.

Without warning, the thick nylon line snagged and parted.

The bomb and parachute were briefly suspended in the inky depths and then, in slow motion, tumbled over and over back down the slope.

The fog of mud screened from Wilson and McCamis the downward plunge of the bomb, but it leap-frogged over the gully, side-stepped the crevice, slithered in the ooze and vanished. The bomb was running away!

The Alvin, its batteries by now almost exhausted, was unable to set off in pursuit. Hopes of recovery looked blacker than ever.

*   *   *

A U.S. Navy communiqué issued at 1800 hours on Sunday, March 27, told the grim story of what had happened. It said: 'Admiral Guest advises that, in a first attempt to recover the object with parachute attached in the waters off Palomares, the lift line parted as a result of having become caught in and cut by the fluke of an anchor which was part of the recovery rig. The object and parachute are still in the same area, but have moved from the position at which they were originally located, making the next recovery attempt even more difficult and lengthy.'

The Aluminaut – following the signals of the transponder – had eventually re-located the hydrogen bomb on a 35 degree slope as slippery as glass. The alarming depth: 2,850 feet.

The warhead had tumbled 300 feet, was in a worse position for possible recovery, and was resting not far from a gaping hole estimated at 4,200 feet deep!

Its position was as precarious as ever. Further rapid modifications to CURV would be necessary for it to reach the warhead before it tumbled further down the slope and was lost for good.

That 'ornery' bomb had won the first round of its battle with the robot, even before the tussle had begun.

CHAPTER ELEVEN

With the fate of the H-bomb still agonisingly in the balance, the sly digs against America continued on a merry old scale. Russia, as usual, led the clamour of protest. In Moscow the Soviet Foreign minister, Andrei Gromyko, cited the Palomares incident and harshly told the United States to get out of Europe.

America – 'a non-European power' – should leave Europe to the Europeans, he asserted in a hard-hitting speech to the 23rd Soviet Party Congress which echoed the sentiments of France's President de Gaulle.

'The United States believes,' he said, 'that Europe cannot do without its presence and trusteeship, bases and soldiers, planes and crews which have reached such a height of perfection that they have started losing hydrogen bombs.'

In Paris, a Communist deputy, Robert Manceau, asked whether the government intended to bar access to French air space to all planes, foreign or French, carrying nuclear weapons.

Defence minister Pierre Messmer claimed that an accident similar to the one at Palomares could not happen in France. In a written reply he said that 'in certain circumstances planes of the French Strategic Air Force make flights with nuclear weapons on board. But every precaution is always taken and there is no risk.

'At the same time, under normal circumstances, overflights of our national territory by foreign planes carrying bombs are forbidden.'

America, however, was no longer meekly sitting back and allowing the propaganda punches to be delivered without crossing a counter blow.

In the United Nations, U.S. ambassador Arthur Goldberg, after his return from the disarmament talks at Geneva, said he had found no indication that the loss of the H-bomb had injured the American position in regard to nuclear non-proliferation.

'I don't think this has hurt the U.S. initiative in the disarmament conference,' said Goldberg. 'There has been some discussion and some things have emerged.

'One is a confirmation that there is no possibility of a nuclear explosion as a result of security measures taken with the aircraft and weapons. The real key to progress is a very essential treaty against nuclear proliferation in which the Soviet Union and Peking – all the nuclear powers – should be ready to agree . . . a treaty which really relates to nuclear proliferation.'

With the bomb stubbornly resisting all the recovery attempts America's position at this time of crisis was unenviable. There was no doubt that if the U.S. Navy was unable to retrieve the weapon, the chorus of political sniping would become a worldwide symphony of protest.

On the other hand, what did America intend to do if the bomb was recovered?

Already, within the Pentagon, there was acute consternation among military leaders to suggestions by civilian chiefs of the Johnson administration that the hydrogen bomb, if raised from the seabed, should be publicly displayed.

Tad Szulc, the respected correspondent in Spain of the New York *Times,* pointed out that the Navy and Air Force commanders on the scene – namely Admiral Guest and General Wilson – strongly opposed any such peepshow on security grounds.

No H-bomb had ever been displayed to the world before. There was another reason, too. The warhead, which rested in the seabed mud, was one of the most modern designed thermonuclear bombs with top-secret 'hardware' – or component parts – in the United States' arsenal.

One of the major political considerations for the U.S. in recovering the weapon, said Szulc, was to establish what officials called 'international credibility.'

Therefore, putting the bomb on show seemed to be the only way in which the U.S. could effectively stifle the mounting Soviet propaganda and charges that the sunken missile might be left for ever near the Spanish coast.

While a compromise was sought in the spirited fight between the civilian and military leaders, efforts to raise the bomb were renewed.

*　　　*　　　*

Reposing on the fantail of the submarine rescue ship Petrel, with its cables, eyes, pipe structure and claw, sat the CURV, ready for action.

Lieutentant-Commander Harrell, captain of the Petrel, stood, hands on hips, by the red egg-shaped submarine rescue bell as the technicians prepared for the robot to be lifted off its cradle and lowered into the Mediterranean.

The electric cable had been duly extended so that on its first dive CURV would be able to explore the seabed up to 3,100 feet below.

The weather on that afternoon of Wednesday, March 30, was cloudy and dull. The winds were again beginning to whip up the white caps and storms were forecast.

Gently, CURV was winched over the side and into the sea. The thick greased cable on a steel rotating drum unwound as the strange vessel disappeared into the blue-green waters on a test dive.

No attempt would be made to raise the bomb on this trip. The electronic technicians had to ensure the cable worked proficiently at its new depth, while the sonar specialist had to find out if the robot would be able to pick up the acoustic signal emitted by the pinger attached to the parachute.

CURV passed both tests with flying colours. The initial dive was to the maximum depth –a record for CURV – and the high resolution sonar bleeped to the surface, loud and clear, its established contact with the bomb.

But hopes of an early recovery were soon to be dashed. The following day rain and choppy seas once more halted the operations.

When the weather finally cleared sufficiently for diving to be resumed on the Friday, the Alvin went down, only to discover that the bomb and parachute had completely disappeared from sight. Both were still roughly at the same spot because the pilots were able to detect the reflected signal from the sonar transponder. But the bomb had been swallowed up by the thick, treacly mud of the slope where it had been nestling.

It was a diabolical situation. The Alvin was unable to probe into the soft slope without sending up clouds of swirling and blinding mud. The television cameras were virtually useless and direct observation was impossible.

The Aluminaut faced the identical problem, and even CURV was beaten by the mud, for it was absolutely essential for its underwater TV to first locate the bomb before a lift line could be attached by its claw.

With this new setback, U.S. officials both in Spain and America clamped down on information although admitting that the recovery 'might now be delayed for weeks.'

The mud into which the bomb and parachute had sunk was virtually an underwater quicksand and there was now a distinct possibility that the warhead had been lost for ever.

But the U.S. Navy refused to admit defeat and doggedly stuck to the task of trying to hook Contact 261 out of the mud.

The bomb's casing, apparently intact, was bearing a crushing pressure of 1,124 pounds per square inch at 2,850 feet. But there was no danger of salt water leaking inside the core or of the nuclear materials seeping out.

To emphasise there was no contamination of the Mediterranean, the fishermen of Garrucha, Villaricos and Aguilas, who had been unable to cast their nets in the waters of Palomares for almost eleven weeks, were told the ban had been lifted.

American scientists were still taking precautionary tests of the water every day, but no traces of radioactivity had yet been found.

And a note from the U.S. embassy in Madrid also stressed there was no hazard from the bomb in the sea. 'The fact is that regardless of the condition of the bomb's case no detectable amount of nuclear materials would spread into the surrounding water. Weapons-grade plutonium and uranium are virtually insoluble. They are very heavy metals and would tend to settle quickly to the bottom in the immediate vicinity of the weapon.

'If scattered, particles suspended in the water would be so widely dispersed and diluted among masses of seawater as to be undetectable to the most sophisticated instruments.

'Any particles which might be ingested by sea life would quickly pass through their systems and be eliminated. Thus, there would be no hazard to sea life, swimmers, or to the sea itself.'

For the next four days Alvin, Aluminaut and CURV vainly continued their efforts to penetrate through the mud of the 30-foot wide quicksand, groping for the bomb with their claws.

rescue rigs and anchor hooks.

'It's a question of patience, endurance and time,' said Admiral Guest, with just a hint of hopelessness in his voice.

Then on the morning of Tuesday, April 5, CURV was once more lowered from the Petrel into the sea. Over an hour later it had reached the muddy slope where the bomb had vanished in the mud. Its mercury vapour lights cut through the black depths and its TV camera blinked inquisitively across the ocean floor.

In the control console aboard the Petrel there was a sudden whoop of triumph. It came from the technicians closely studying the grey blurred pictures flashed up through the cable on to the television screen.

There they were. Unmistakably. The lazily flapping folds of a parachute, looking like a sleeping sea anemone just awakened.

Lieutenant-Commander Harrell sent an urgent message to Admiral Guest in the plotting room of the Albany.

The tricky manoeuvre was started to try and attach a lift line. CURV hovered determinedly over its target, lights blazing from the tubular frame and with the cable – a flimsy but vital link with the surface control – disappearing into the darkness above.

The jaws of the hydraulically operated claw gaped wide open as its motors propelled CURV down to within two feet of the parachute. The claw, right in front of the camera lens, hungrily ate into the mass of billowing silk, snapped shut, and slowly the robot was backed off as though admiring its captured prey.

A recovery buoy was released and amid a hiss of bubbles began its ascent. The ejected claw toppled sideways. Would it come adrift? No, it still grasped the parachute tightly.

For the first time in the 21 days since it had been located by the Alvin it seemed that there was a chance of hauling up the H-bomb directly from the mud.

Instructions went out for CURV to be winched aboard the Petrel, its work successfully completed.

Now the Alvin would be sent down in a bid to secure a second line of braided nylon five-eighths of an inch in diameter and with a breaking strain of 10,800 pounds.

That afternoon the two pilots, Wilson and McCamis, eased themselves into the sub in which they had shared the dramas and perils of 145 dives, repeatedly staying on the bottom in excess of the normal safety margin of eight hours.

For them it was to be a nightmarish dive. The Alvin was towed out of the well deck of the Fort Snelling and guided to the little bobbing buoy marking the spot where the bomb lay fathoms below. Ninety minutes later the two pilots were peering through the large observation window on the Alvin's conning tower, trying once more to discern the bomb and its parachute in the gloom.

Visibility was not particularly good, about six feet, and they had to exercise extreme care in steering their tiny craft to avoid colliding either with the mud slope or with the parachute.

Several times the Alvin moved forward in these murky conditions, grappling claw at the ready, to try and attach the second line. Each attempt failed.

With each run towards the sunken weapon they noticed something strange. At first they were mystified. Then they realised what it was.

The bomb was on the move.

Wilson and McCamis were horrified to observe that it appeared to be sliding down the 35 degree slope on the ooze, slipping nearer and nearer to the gaping hole, 4,200 feet deep.

Quick calculations disclosed that during the last 30 hours in which it had been buried in the mud the bomb had moved 300 feet west-southwest across the seabed. And it was still in motion.

If it was propelled much more by the shifting undersea currents it would slither beyond the mechanical grasp of the Alvin and drop into the chasm.

The chances of the single line attached by CURV being able to take the strain of the bomb, although registering only 1,600 pounds, were slim. During a lift, the parachute was bound to billow out, adding hundreds of pounds of dead weight and probably snapping the line. Or else the line could snag on a subterranean rock or catch on the rescue rig and break, as it had done on the previous occasion.

It became another against-the-clock attempt to hook on the second line. Wilson and McCannis steered daringly to within six feet of the half-buried weapon but ran headlong into the folds of the parachute. They were ensnared 2,850 feet down on the seabed.

It was a deadly situation. The sub could remain on the seabed for only four more hours at the most before its batteries became exhausted. If it struggled to shake free it might become even more tangled up in the shrouds. And the ships above were powerless to help.

A coded alert from Wilson to the surface controller, Mr Rainnie, warned: 'Alvin to control. We are entangled with Robert and completely covered.' The minutes ticked away with no more messages from the deep.

The crew of the Alvin were blinded and helpless. The craft was practically enveloped by the parachute, as if trapped inside a tightly pegged tent with the flaps stitched shut. The internal lights had to be switched off to conserve power.

Wilson and McCamis realised that, with help unable to reach them from above, they faced death in the parachute and its shrouds. Something had to be done and quickly. Wilson took a chance. He steered the Alvin right. It moved. Slowly, tensely, miraculously he extricated the sub inch by inch from the imprisoning shrouds. At last, it was clear.

Wilson and McCamis, wearily acknowledging their luck after the brush with death, slowly re-surfaced. But the pilots would not have much time for recuperation or sleep. The batteries would be given a booster charge, then the next morning Alvin would dive again.

Wednesday dawned with more bad weather, threatening to paralyse the operation, but despite a 22-knot wind and five-foot seas, the Aluminaut, later pursued by the Alvin, went down to try and fix a second braided nylon line to the still-creeping bomb.

Gamely the civilian crews continued their perilous task. And at 10.0 a.m., by sheer determination, came long-sought success. A second line was hooked, strategically, into the top of the parachute to prevent it billowing again.

The troubles, however, were by no means over. Fate rudely intervened, yet again. Because of the rough weather the subs had to be recalled and the recovery bid suspended for ten hours. At 8.0 p.m. there was little improvement and the operation had to be postponed until midnight.

The break gave the fatigued crews of the Alvin and Aluminaut, who had been up for over 30 hours, an opportunity to snatch some sleep.

That evening, with Task Force 65 poised for the big catch, Admiral Guest went aboard the Petrel and the submarine rescue ship, with CURV aboard, moved into the area of the target.

This was Holy Week in strict Roman Catholic Spain, and on Maundy Thursday morning, April 7, CURV, silhouetted by a blaze of searchlights from the circling fleet of warships, was lowered into the water to submerge at 1.30 a.m.

Its task was to try and attach just one more lift line. Then the bomb would be well and truly hooked for safe recovery.

At 3.15 a.m. there were shouts of alarm from the control console aboard the Petrel. The TV pictures transmitted from CURV clearly showed that the robot had also fouled the parachute. The electronic technicians tried everything to free CURV – by vibrating the cable, ejecting the claw, and rotating the craft – but it was impossible. The only consolation was that CURV was an unmanned vehicle.

The bomb kept restlessly on the move as the two attached lines, with the additional ton weight of CURV, became dangerously taut. They were hurriedly secured to the winch boom on the Petrel, normally used for lowering and raising the submarine rescue bell, and shortly before 7.0 a.m., with CURV still trapped, Admiral Guest made the most crucial decision of his command.

'We have to take the weapon now, before it is too late,' he said.

While the weather held reasonably fair, the admiral ordered that an attempt should be made to try and haul up the whole conglomeration – H-bomb, parachute, CURV and all. He gambled on the two braided nylon lines, whose strength was bound to be reduced by 75 per cent because of the turbulent undersea conditions, holding . . .

The ship's boom was prepared to take the strain on the two lines and the electrical cable of CURV.

The sun, pale yellow, rose meekly on the distant horizon, and, although it was chilly, Admiral Guest, with a thick stubble on his chin, sweated freely. Turning to Lieutenant-Commander Harrell he wiped his brow and remarked: 'I would prefer combat any day to this.'

The tension was terrific. The first stages of the lift were the most vital. There was no knowing what would happen to the parachute. After so many days in salt water, the material might have rotted, making it liable to tear easily, and thus the lift-lines could break free.

There was also the risk that vibration would snap the lift-lines, as well as the ever-present danger that if the wet nylon was brought across jagged metal or rock it would part.

'Commence lifting!'

The boom swung out from the side of the Petrel, and the drums with the nylon lines creaked as they slowly began rotating. The lines, as they took the strain, came wet and dripping from the sea, inch by tremulous inch.

Below, the stick-in-the-mud H-bomb was reluctant to leave the comfort of the seabed. The ooze clung to it for an age until suddenly, in a cloud of blinding silt and seaweed, it was torn free – to hang lazily beneath the tangled folds of the parachute and the imprisoned robot.

Up it came. Slowly. Gingerly. Surely.

For over an hour – hoisted at the rate of 27 feet per minute – the hydrogen bomb was raised.

Then, at 8.19, came crisis. CURV had somehow managed to disentangle itself from the parachute. Instantly, it was dragged completely clear. By a miracle, it did not snag the lift-lines. The bomb lift continued.

Lieutenant-Commander Moody, and his team of SCUBA divers, stood by to take down wires and inspect the bomb. Tortuously it was raised to just 100 feet from the surface. Then, through the heaving swell, the spawning shape of the grimy parachute could be seen, while underneath, the shining metal of the bomb itself was discernable.

A black rubber dingly was paddled out from the Petrel to the spot where the lines stretched rigidly from the boom into the sea. Down dived the SCUBA experts. More wires were strapped round the belly of Contact 261.

For almost 15 minutes the dark shapes of divers in rubber suits and flippers, with oxygen bottles strapped on to their backs, could be observed flitting about in the dark Mediterranean blueness below.

Then they re-surfaced. One of the divers gave a thumbs-up sign towards the anxious faces peering down from the deck rails of the Petrel. All was set for the H-bomb to be hauled aboard.

At precisely 8.45, the big silvery bomb, ten feet long and sporting a number of barnacles, was triumphantly lifted out of the sea. From the moment it had plunged down from the stricken B-52 it had been hidden for exactly 79 days, 22 hours and 23 minutes.

Its recovery was an incredible feat – the greatest underwater rescue operation of all time – although the lift itself had taken only one hour and 45 minutes. Gently the weapon was lowered by the boom on to a waiting cradle placed on a Polythene covering on the aft deck. The sodden parachute was draped over its tail.

There it sat, majestic and intact, apart from a few dents inflicted after it had bounced twice on the seabed on the day of the crash.

Admiral Guest and the haggard and weary crew of the Petrel, stood in an admiring semi-circle to view their catch. It seemed fantastic that this snub-nosed bomb was capable of killing thousands of people and wreaking havoc and destruction on the world.

'Thank God, we finally did it!' commented the relieved Admiral. Ashore, General Wilson had been alerted and with Air Force explosive ordnance disposal technicians, was already on his way formally to identify the bomb.

The Navy and Air Force bomb experts, in white protective clothing, rubber gloves, plastic covered boots, masks and breathing apparatus strapped to their chests, moved in cautiously to make routine checks with alpha scintillation meters. There was no leakage of plutonium or uranium.

Then a series of electrical plugs were carefully disconnected, and the inner TNT detonating charge defused.

At 10.14 it was announced to Admiral Guest that the bomb had 'fallen safe.'

'We were very happy indeed,' he reflected. 'There wasn't much backslapping. We were too tired.'

The Admiral then relayed the news to the U.S. embassy in Madrid, after waiting nearly two hours before announcing the triumph, 'to make damn sure I had it.'

At noon came the official communiqué: 'The fourth and final weapon from the January 17 crash near Palomares has been recovered today and will be transported directly to the

United States. The casing was intact. The weapon was located, on March 15, in 2,500 feet of water, approximately five miles off shore, by units of Task Force 65. Photographs taken at that time tentatively identified the object as the missing weapon. The recovery of this weapon brings to a close the search phase of the operation. No release of radioactivity into the coastal waters has occurred. All wreckage fragments and associated aircraft material of interest to the accident investigation have now been located and recovered.'

In America, Mr McNamara, the Defence Secretary, was notified of the recovery, and in turn informed Mr Rusk, the Secretary of State, and President Johnson. The military chiefs at the Pentagon were jubilant.

They still battled spiritedly against a public display of the nuclear bomb but eventually a compromise was reached.

The following day the world was, for the first time, to be given just a glimpse of an H-bomb. Spanish officials, together with international Press and TV units, would be invited aboard the flagship Albany for a parade past of the Petrel, with the warhead displayed at rest on its fantail.

CHAPTER TWELVE

'L A Bomba es recuperada!' shouted the villagers of Palomares.
'The Americans have pulled it up!'

One Madrid newspaper declared that the recovery was a
Holy Week 'miracle.'

In Cuevas de Almanzora the parish priest, Father Enrique
Arriaga, said simply: 'It is the work of God himself.'

Fisherman Francisco Simo drank a glass of celebration wine
with his crew at Agulias when he heard the news on the radio.
'I am very happy that I was able to give a little help,' was his
modest comment.

At 9.0 a.m. that Good Friday, after a ten hour drive from
Madrid in which my car was stuck in the middle of religious
processions at a number of tiny villages, I was back at Palomares.

This time I drove on to Garrucha, where lined up in the
harbour were a number of flag-draped U.S. Navy vessels waiting
to take us out to keep the appointment with an H-bomb.

Half-an-hour later I was on the gently heaving deck of the
cruiser Albany for America's peepshow of a hydrogen bomb
that could flatten any city in the world.

Hundreds of sailors in their best blue lined the decks of the
cruiser as the Petrel steamed up for the parade-past on the starboard side.

For ten minutes, the Petrel was inched to within 15 yards of
the Albany. The lethal bomb looked innocent enough – ten feet
long, a canister shaped like the silver foil container of a
good quality Havana cigar, laid out on a cradle on the aft deck
behind two huge rust-stained anchors (see cover photo). The
folds of the parachute had been carefully arranged to hide any
top-secret information that the eye might be able to detect.

Small strips of white masking tape had been patched over
various parts of the bomb to obscure classified data. The nose
and tail dents were plainly visible. So, too, was the yellow metal
harness to which the parachute was attached.

184

Four Marines, armed with Colt .45's, and one with a riot rifle slung casually across his folded arms, stood smartly to attention round the bomb, like a guard of honour.

After the weeks of strain and tension there had to be informality. Two civilians, in bright red sweat shirts, clasped their hands above their heads in jubilation and Admiral Guest pointed down at the bomb and leaned forward to pat it affectionately on the nose.

It seemed strange to be inspecting an H-bomb on Good Friday. On shore, thousands of impoverished villagers for miles around were oblivious to the bomb and knelt in the streets in prayer. Ornate religious floats, depicting Christ carrying the Cross, were hauled to the beat of muffled drums through the cobbled alleyways by penitents wearing mauve hooded robes, like the white robes worn by Ku Klux Klansmen, and some with their ankles chained. For the Spaniards, it was the most religious day of the year and the drama of living with a bomb a few miles from their backdoors was temporarily forgotten.

Yet here were we on the Albany, at times it seemed, almost paying homage to the most awesome weapon ever invented by man.

In the background, behind the Petrel, the three gaily coloured submersibles – Aluminaut, Alvin and Cubmarine – which at times had faced disaster during the hunt, bobbed in the sea clear of the thrashing propellers.

Only the continuous whirr of television cameras, and the click of shutters, broke the silence as the Petrel edged in to give the world a close-up.

On the aft deck alongside the bomb was a huge blue-painted metal container or 'coffin' into which the weapon would eventually be buried in fine sand. Coffin and bomb would then weigh a hefty 16,000 lbs.

Then it was all over. Admiral Guest boarded a tiny launch to return to his flagship and the Petrel steamed away with the bomb glinting dully in the morning sunshine as it disappeared from sight. Soon it would be packed into its coffin for the trans-Atlantic crossing.

America's lost H-bomb had been retrieved, reluctantly leaving its hiding place in the sea and within 48 hours would be on its way home.

For Admiral Guest there was yet another ordeal to be faced –
that of explaining to the world how the remarkable feat of raising
the bomb had been achieved.

The stocky, sandy-haired Admiral was rocking with weariness
and his eyes were red through lack of sleep as he faced a battery
of TV cameras and questions in the wardroom of the Albany.

He patiently related details of the recovery drama just over
24 hours before, and of the vital role played by the civilians –
the fisherman Senor Simo, the pilots of the Alvin, Wilson and
McCamis, and their surface controller, Mr Rainnie.

'This fisherman was extremely helpful in establishing the
area where the bomb was eventually located and has been out
with the Task Force on three occasions,' he explained. 'I cannot
say enough for the crew of the Alvin. They are not military
personnel. They are civilians whose only interest was in doing
a job for their country.

'My outfit was magnificent. The crew of the Petrel, like my-
self, have not slept for two nights and managed to get only three
hours sleep on a third night.'

Why was the bomb being transported back on a ship? 'One
reason is because it is very, very heavy in its coffin.'

Could the bomb still be used? 'I would not want to put in on
a plane with those dents in it!'

Have black boxes from the B-52, containing top-secret codes,
also been recovered from the sea? 'It is true that items of
classified equipment have been retrieved from the seabed but
I am not allowed to give details for security reasons.'

Is there still anything important to be recovered from the
Mediterranean? 'Anyone who wants to pick up anything on the
bottom can sure as Hell have it. It's not worth anything.'

Did you ever feel like quitting the long and seemingly hopeless
search? 'No sir! I don't think like that when I am told to go
and pick up a weapon.'

Has useful knowledge been gained as a result of the sea hunt?
'We've learnt more on deep submergence than in any single
operation that has ever taken place before. Every scientist and
researcher here has been in Seventh Heaven.'

Why was the bomb so valuable to warrant an 80-day search?
'The bomb was valuable not only because of its hardware but
because of its important design.'

Was there any danger of a nuclear blast? 'None whatsoever.'

Throughout the 90-minute conference the Admiral stumbled hoarsely over his words, wearily wiped his brow, and once remarked: 'I'm bushed.'

Suppose the attempt had failed? What would have happened then? Do you think anyone else could have found and recovered the weapon? 'I believe we mobilised the best scientific talent and equipment in the world today. I don't think anyone else could have done it. Nobody has recovered anything of this weight at such a depth before.'

Were you worried by the presence of the Russian ship? 'There are Soviet trawlers in many waters of the world and the one lurking in the general area of the search never ventured too close. I doubt if the Russians learned anything and they certainly could not have recovered the bomb under our noses.'

Has the search now ended? 'Yes. Mission completed!'

The applause for the Admiral, as he finished his marathon conference, was spontaneous. Ambassador Mr Duke summed up everyone's feelings when he remarked: 'You have the gratitude of the world.'

*　　　*　　　*

So, at last, it was all over bar the shouting. And this time the shouts were those of praise.

Admittedly, Moscow suggested the recovery was just a hoax with Soviet newspaper headlines sceptically asking: 'Has the bomb really been recovered?'

But, rightly, the plaudits came flooding in.

Mr McNamara, the Defence Secretary, congratulated everyone – military personnel and civilians – whose efforts had transformed a tragic accident into 'a clear demonstration of a responsible nation acting in good faith.'

He said: 'The recovery of the missing nuclear weapon brings to a conclusion a critical phase of an extremely difficult and vitally important task.'

The State Department finally delivered the long-overdue knockout punch to flatten the Russian propaganda charges. From Mr Rusk's office in Washington came this official commentary:

'The Soviet Union, which has been trying to make propaganda gains from the incident right along, has hinted that the weapon was not really found or raised. Since the weapon has now been publicly displayed and the full details of how it was raised given out, the Soviet charge has been pretty effectively demolished.

'There will no doubt be a general feeling of relief that the weapon has been found, for many people persisted in thinking that it could somehow go off by itself. The chances of this, however, were so remote as to be virtually non-existent. It could happen only if a whole series of safety devices – mechanical and electronic locks – were unlocked in exactly the right sequence, which is highly unlikely. As scientists have repeatedly pointed out, there have been several accidents involving nuclear weapons in the past ten years – most of them in the United States – and none has ever resulted in a nuclear explosion. Tests have actually been conducted in which nuclear weapons were put into tanks of burning oil and others slammed into concrete walls at 1,500 m.p.h. In every case, the device refused to explode.'

Honours, medals and rewards for the men who played a leading role in the H-bomb hunt were soon to follow.

America presented to Francisco Simo, on April 15, a medal and a diploma 'as a testimony to the exceptional talent and deep knowledge of the sea which led to the finding of the nuclear bomb.' The fisherman hero of Spain, it was announced on June 21, was also to receive his country's highest naval award, the Naval Cross of Merit. And a popular nationwide fund was opened to buy him a new, £36,000 fishing boat.

The Spanish and U.S. commanders of the 'Broken Arrow' land operation were also honoured.

General Montel Pouzet was awarded the Legion of Merit by U.S. Air Secretary Harold Brown, in Madrid, on May 13, as a token of the gratitude of the American government for the Spanish co-operation at Palomares.

General Wilson, succeeded by General Donovan as Commander of the 16th Air Force at Torrejon prior to his retirement, was awarded the Distinguished Service Medal, America's highest peace time decoration. The medal, presented on May 27, by Lieutenant General Richard M. Montgomery, Deputy Commander-in-Chief of the U.S. Air Force in Europe, was accompanied by a citation stating that 'General Wilson's demonstration of outstanding diplomacy and superior direction resulted in the United States attaining a new level of trust, confidence and respect from senior Spanish officials with regard to the Palomares incident.'

For Task Force 65 commander, Admiral Guest, there were the congratulations of all the U.S. Navy's top brass, from the Secretary of the Navy and the Commander-in-Chief of the U.S. Naval Forces in Europe, to Admiral Ellis, the Commander of the Sixth Fleet, who had originally selected him to lead the sea hunt.

In Washington, the U.S. Navy totted up the cost of the deep-sea salvage operation in which 18 ships and 3,800 men had been involved, and said it would amount to 'several million dollars.' Unofficial estimates calculate the cost of the entire job – land, sea and air – at a shock £30 million.

No wonder that a month after the bomb had been raised and America had paid its heavy price for the B-52 disaster – financially and politically – it was announced by Mr McNamara that he was drastically reducing the airborne alert by bombers of the Strategic Air Command.

The decision, undoubtedly accelerated by the lesson of Palomares, reflected the growing importance of intercontinental missiles and, as McNamara put it 'the declining importance of manned bombers.'

He said the joint Chiefs of Staff 'objected to eliminating all of the air alert.' Consequently, a reduced B-52 force would continue to man global patrols – but without additional financial aid. The force would certainly never aspire to its heights of power again, as it had during the 1962 Cuba missile crisis, when, at times, 90 per cent of the U.S. Air Force bombers had been airborne.

'The bomber alert,' said McNamara, 'provides us with only a small capability and it has become particularly small in relation to our huge and growing missile force.'

Meanwhile, the dirt described by the Atomic Energy Commission as 'mildly contaminated', had been duly buried after its sea journey to Charleston, and a 120-mile trip by freight train to the nuclear graveyard at the Savannah River plant, near Aiken. The poisoned earth – like that similarly bulldozed under the ground at the A.E.C.'s other sites at Hanford, near Richland,

Washington, at Oak Ridge, near Knoxsville, Tennessee, and at Idaho Falls, Idaho – would be continually monitored for radioactivity.

With the wayward H-bomb home and dissected by the scientists to discover the effects of almost 80 days in salt water, the expected lifting of the ban against U.S. nuclear flights over Spain did not immediately materialise.

However, a reversal of Madrid policy was indicated by the granting of permission to the U.S. to base three squadrons of N.A.T.O.-assigned F-100 jetfighters at Torrejon. The 54 planes were transferred from bases in Italy and Turkey in a big re-shuffle to the U.S. Air Force defences in Europe, necessitated by the intended withdrawal from and eviction of N.A.T.O. by France's go-it-alone de Gaulle.

It was now clear that Generalissimo Franco's clamp-down on the overflights immediately following the B-52 crash had not upset the cordial relations between Spain and America. He had been uncannily correct in assuming that the U.S. would seek to station more of its military personnel in Spain as a result of the N.A.T.O. crisis. Altogether in France there were 15,750 Army, 250 Navy and more than 14,000 Air Force personnel who would have to be found new bases in Western Europe by April 1, 1967 – de Gaulle's deadline for the Americans to get out of France. Spain was one of the more obvious choices.

The clanger of the dropped H-bombs had not weakened ties between the two countries after all. On the contrary, it had strengthened them.

*　　*　　*

Today, life is almost back to normal at sleepy Palomares although – like the rest of the world – the villagers will never completely forget. When the bomb was still being sought at sea, most of the land-based airmen, G.I.s and sailors had packed their gear and loaded it on buses, trucks and landing craft, to return home. Villagers had then turned out in force to give them a fond adios. The warmth of the farewell was in striking contrast to the initial suspicion and muttered resentment which the Americans had encountered on arrival.

The U.S. 16th Air Force band, flown down specially from Torrejon, added some pomp to the occasion and had serenaded the villagers at a closing ceremony at the tent city on the sands. There were tears of nostalgia in the eyes of some Spaniards at seeing the men and machines who had made their simple lives so suddenly complicated, pull up stakes and disappear. Left behind were bare tent sites, myriads of lorry and caterpillar tracks and scores of empty crates of tomatoes consumed by the troops.

General Wilson handed over 72,000 pesetas – almost £430 – donated by his men towards the building of a new church at Palomares. The local businessmen had prospered during the two months of American occupation. The owner of a big petrol station at nearby Vera had paid off a £600 debt, a storekeeper had sold out of his entire stock of the locally-worn black berets adopted by the troops, and a taxi driver, counting an impressive bundle of money, remarked: 'We could almost stand another small bomb.'

Then – as suddenly as they had arrived – the Americans were gone from dusty Palomares for good. The village with no telephones, no roads and only one television set, which had found itself unwillingly propelled into the twentieth century on a sunny morning in January, now found itself restored to its former tranquil state.

But the 1,200 humble inhabitants retained one nagging fear, a question that even today remains unanswered.

How will the stigma of having had H-bombs plummet into their fields and mildly contaminate their crops affect their futures?

Only time will provide an answer. Certainly the scientists – American and Spanish alike – will not allow the people of Palomares to forget easily.

They will be back in a year's time to make routine tests of the soil, the animals and the new crops. They will be back in five years, ten years and beyond George Orwell's 1984.

Maybe, by then, the fervent wish of some of the villagers will have been realised and Palomares will be a booming tourist centre.

The day of the bombs, however, will never be completely forgotten. Palomares might have been pronounced 'surgically clean' but no matter how scrupulously the scientists have undertaken the task of decontamination it is an indisputable fact that unknown quantities of plutonium 239 and uranium 235 were scattered around the region in dust storms and escaped detection.

There will, of course, be not the slightest danger as a result of this. Any radioactivity lurking behind can be blocked by a piece of paper.

But Palomares has inevitably acquired a reputation – and reputations have a nasty habit of sticking.

*　　　*　　　*

The U.S. Air Force still maintains a skeleton patrol of nuclear-armed bombers. At any hour of any day the whistle of jet engines in the sky above could be the prelude to a similar H-bomb disaster like the one in Spain.

It must not be forgotten that there have now been thirteen known accidents involving nuclear weapons of the U.S. Air Force in eight years. There will assuredly be another disaster – another Palomares. More accidents are bound to occur so long as the giant bombers continue to take off and land at the Strategic Air Command bases.

Perhaps, one day, the still-missing bomb which was swallowed up over five years ago by a swamp, after a B-52 crashed 15 miles north of the Seymour Johnson Air Force base, at Goldsboro, will also be recovered! But, indisputably, the best mechanics in the world cannot promise that an aircraft carrying nuclear bombs will never crash on foreign soil again. The next time it happens might be in Britain, in Germany, in Holland – or in other countries of Western Europe, Asia, Africa and Latin America.

And not even the most brilliant scientists are prepared to rule out entirely the possibility of an accidental blast. Otherwise, why are these awesome bombs still submitted to such tests as plunging them in burning oil, slamming them into brick walls or submerging them for months at a time?

That is why the story of Palomares has no real end.

Madrid, August, 1966.